INTRODUCT

TO

CURRY

CURRY POWDER AND SPICE MIXES

HEALTH BENEFITS AND RECIPES

JOSEPH VEEBE

Copyright © 2017-2020 by Joseph Veebe. All Rights Reserved.

Print ISBN: 9781717908568

E-Book ASIN: B07FRV1B6N

No part of this publication may be reproduced, distributed, or transmitted in any form or by any means, including photocopying, recording, or other electronic or mechanical methods, or by any information storage and retrieval system without the prior written permission of the publisher, except in the case of very brief quotations embodied in critical reviews and certain other noncommercial uses permitted by copyright law.

CURRY: Curry Powder and Spice Mixes

Books in this Series:

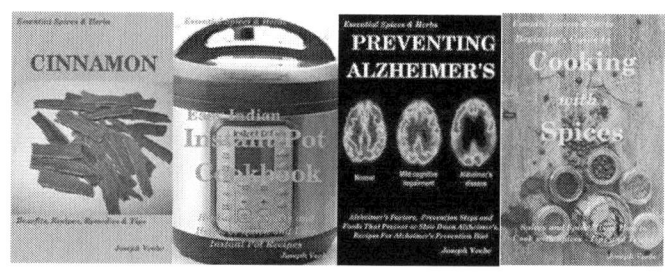

CURRY: Curry Powder and Spice Mixes

TABLE OF CONTENTS

Table of Contents 3
Chapter 1. Introduction 7
    Introduction 7
    Origin 8
Chapter 2. Ingredients For Curry Powder and Spice Mixes .. 14
Chapter 3. Curry Powder And Spice Mix Recipes 22
    Recipe #1: Quick and Easy Mild Curry Powder 22
    Recipe #2: Spicy Curry Powder 23
    Recipe #3: Mild Curry Powder 24
    Recipe #4: Very Mild Red Curry Powder 25
    Recipe #5: Basic Thai Red Curry Paste 26
    Recipe #6: Thai Green Curry Paste 27
    Recipe #7: Thai Yellow Curry Paste 28
    Recipe #8: Indian Curry Paste 28
    Recipe #9: Garam Masala 30
    Recipe #10: Ethiopian Berbere Mix 31
    Recipe #11: Jamaican Curry Powder 31
    Other Spice Blends 33
Chapter 4. Health Benefits Of Curry Powder 35
    Reducing Inflammation 35
    Antioxidant Properties 36
    Fighting Cancer 38
    Fighting Alzheimer's Disease 39
    Parkinson's 40

CURRY: Curry Powder and Spice Mixes

Lower Blood Pressure 41

Neuro-protective 41

Diabetes and Heart Health 42

Cholesterol 43

Indigestion, Bloating, Constipation, IBS 44

Immune System & Infections 45

Pain and Arthritis 46

Improved Circulation 47

Chapter 5. Cooking With Curry Powder And Spice Mixes 48

Bell Pepper And Chicken Stir Fry 48

Coconut Curry Chicken 49

Beef/Chicken Pepper Fry 51

Cauliflower And Potato Curry 52

Potato Curry 53

Quick Fish Curry With Canned Tuna 54

Bell Pepper Curry 56

Simplified Chicken Curry Recipe #1 57

Simplified Chicken Curry Recipe #2 58

Simplified Chicken Curry Recipe #3 60

Egg Curry Recipe #1 (simple version) 61

Egg Curry Recipe #2 63

Lentil Curry Recipes 64

Lentil Curry Recipe #1 (simple version) 66

Lentil Curry Recipe #2 67

Lentil And Spinach Curry 68

Quick And Easy Chickpeas Curry 69

CURRY: Curry Powder and Spice Mixes

Quick and Easy Canned Garbanzo Beans Curry 70
Easy Thai Red Curry Chicken 70
Easy Thai Red Curry vegetables 71
Mutton Curry Recipe #1 73
Mutton Curry Recipe #2 74
Thai Coconut Curry Noodle Soup (chicken) 76
Thai Coconut Curry Noodle Soup (vegan) 77
Quick And Easy Doro Wat (Ethiopian Chicken Curry) . 78
Eggplant Curry (Vegan) 80
Mixed Vegetable Curry (Vegan) 81
Vegetable Korma 82
Thai Green Curry Chicken 89
Thai Pork And Peanut Curry 90
Street Food Style Spicy Chicken Curry 91
Butter Chicken 93
Chicken Tikka Masala 95
Simple Creamed Spinach (palak) Curry 97
References 99
Disclaimer 100

Preview of Other Books in this Series 102
Essential Spices and Herbs: Turmeric 102
Preventing Cancer 103
Preventing Alzheimer's 104
All Natural Wellness Drinks 106
Essential Spices and Herbs: Ginger 106
Essential Spices and Herbs: Garlic 107

CURRY: Curry Powder and Spice Mixes

Essential Spices and Herbs: Cinnamon 108

Anti-Cancer Curries 108

Beginners Guide to Cooking with Spices 109

Easy Indian Instant Pot Cookbook 110

Fighting the Virus: How to Boost Your Body's Immune Response and Fight Virus Naturally 110

Easy Spicy Eggs: All Natural Easy and Spicy Egg Recipes 111

Food for the Brain 112

CURRY: Curry Powder and Spice Mixes

CHAPTER 1. INTRODUCTION

INTRODUCTION

Curry is usually an Indian dish made of meat, fish or vegetables cooked with spices and herbs. The end product is that the cooked meat, fish, or vegetables are fully soaked in a savory spicy sauce. Curry is usually eaten with rice or bread. The dish is very colorful – most often red or yellow and in some cases, green.

Curry powder or Indian curry powder is a mix of several spices, in some cases up to 20 different spices and herbs. The most notable spices used are coriander, cumin, turmeric, and chili powder. Other ingredients may include cardamom, cinnamon, black pepper, ground ginger, ground mustard, fenugreek, nutmeg, and fennel. By varying the proportion of these spices, one can create mild, medium, or hot curry powder with distinct taste differences as well as health benefits.

Besides Indian curry, there are many other variants of curry from other countries such as Japanese curry, Thai curry, Ethiopian curry, and many others.

The spices and herbs used in curry are known for many health benefits including anti-cancer, anti-inflammatory, anti-oxidant, and many others. Curry, therefore, is an excellent health food and should be incorporated into your food habits and diet regime.

One can make their own curry powder by mixing various spice powders or blending various whole spices. This offers a lot of flexibility in terms of controlling the spice and heat level as well as going with the spices one likes or are more beneficial and avoid or limit others. Many recipes for making spice blends for curry powder are included in this book.

If one wants to go for pre-packaged curry powders or curry paste, there are many options available on the market. You may want to choose carefully as no two recipes for the packaged curry powder are the same. Pre-packaged curry powder and paste are available in many South Asian and Indian stores as well as online stores such as Amazon.

ORIGIN

Spice blends were used in cooking during the days of Indus Valley Civilization, almost 4000 years ago as many spices were cultivated in the Indian subcontinent. The locals mixed and matched these spices in the preparation of food. Mostly, these spices were used to enhance food flavor or to increase the shelf life of the prepared food as no refrigeration or another modern food preservation was available. Over time, these ancient civilizations recognized that these spice blends have health benefits beyond flavoring or preserving food.

While the use of spice blends dates 4000 years ago, the idea of "curry" powder came from the 18th-century English colonists who were part of the South Asian spice trade. English colonists did not quite understand the local population's preparation and use of spice blends. They called anything prepared using a spice blend, "curry".

The word "curry" originated from the word "*Kari*" which means "sauce or relish for rice" in Tamil, a language spoken in the southern part of India, Sri Lanka, and parts of southeast Asia.

Variations of Indian curry powder

While curry powder is a more generic form of spice blend, there are several variations available in the market.

Regular curry powder contains more turmeric, coriander, and cumin and is more yellow in color.

Madras curry powder is typically a spicier version and contains more chili powder (therefore redder in color) in the blend.

Hot curry powder, like Madras curry powder, has extra kick due to the added chili powder or a hotter version of the chili used in addition to ginger powder.

Maharaja curry powder is rich, mild, and sweet and perfumed by the use of saffron and cardamom.

Sweet curry powder is the mildest and maybe the right spice mix for someone who is starting with curry powder. Sweet curry powder contains less chili, more turmeric, and other mild spices.

Other spice mixes used to make curries

Garam Masala

Garam Masala, which literally means "hot spice", is a spice mix of north Indian origin. It is not considered curry powder, but sometimes is used along with curry powder or occasionally used as a substitute. Garam masala typically includes coriander, cumin, cinnamon, nutmeg, cloves, and peppercorns among other things. Garam masala has a bit more pungent flavor than curry powder.

Sambhar powder

Sambhar (or Saambaar, Saambar) is a lentil-based stew or soup cooked in tamarind broth and seasoned with Sambhar powder. This is a popular dish in South India and Sri Lanka. Sambhar is often eaten as a soup or with south Indian dishes such as idli (steamed rice cake) or dosa (lentil crepes) or just plain cooked rice. As with curry powder, there are many variations of Sambhar masala you can buy on the market. There are many variations in the preparation of Sambhar dish as well.

Biriyani masala

Biriyani masala is not strictly used to make curries but is a spice mix for making seasoned rice mixed with meat (chicken, mutton, beef, prawn, or fish) or vegetables. Biriyani masala also comes in many varieties and often indicative of the locality or origin of the dish. The spice mixes, as well as modes of preparation, vary according to the place it originated (e.g. Hyderabadi, Malabar, Bombay, Karachi) as well the type of meat or vegetable used.

Rasam powder

Rasam is a South Indian soup (similar to Sambhar but much lighter and thinner) that is based on tamarind or tomato and seasoned with black pepper, cumin, chili powder, and other seasonings. It is typically eaten with cooked rice or most often as a spicy soup that is well known as a remedy to clear a stuffy nose, mild headache, and flu symptoms.

Chaat masala

Chaat masala (or chat masala) is a mild spice mix consisting of dried mango powder, cumin, black pepper, coriander, and dried ginger (and some other spices depending on taste). It is originated in South Asia and is usually sprinkled on fruits, toasts, and salads. The chaat masala is also sprinkled on snacks sold by vendors on the streets of Mumbai, Delhi, and other north Indian (primarily) cities.

Vindaloo masala

Vindaloo is a type of curry but is distinguished as Portuguese influenced cuisine from the state of Goa in India. In a traditional Goan cuisine, the meat is usually marinated in vinegar, ginger, garlic, and other spices overnight before cooking. Vindaloo masala typically contains red chilies, cumin, cinnamon, cardamom, cloves, black pepper, tomato paste, and/or vinegar.

Japanese Curry mix/paste

Curry became a popular dish in Japan after the British introduced it in the 19th century. Japanese adapted the Indian curry and it became one of Japan's national dishes. Japanese curry powder is a mild version of Indian curry powder. However, the preparation of Japanese curry is quite different than that of Indian curry. Japanese curry is not usually very spicy but is a bit sweet and savory in taste and thick in texture. While you can use a mild version of curry spice recipe in this book to make Japanese curry (rice), there are a number of Japanese curry blends are available in the market such as Vermont curry, Java curry, and Torokeru curry.

Thai Curry mix/paste

Thai curry refers to dishes made with Thai curry paste. Thai curry can be made with meat, seafood, vegetables or tofu. One of my all-time favorite Thai dishes is roasted duck curry. Thai curry paste differs from Indian curry powder or paste due to the type of ingredients added. The typical ingredients in Thai curry paste include red chilies, coriander, onions/shallots, lemongrass, lime, shrimp paste, fish sauce, garlic, and ginger or galangal. Ingredients such as turmeric, cumin, black pepper, cardamom, and others may be added depending on the main ingredient for the curry dish – such as meat, seafood, or vegetables. Many of the Thai curry dishes use coconut milk as the base.

Thai curry comes in 3 distinct flavors, Thai red curry, Thai yellow curry, and Thai green curry.

Thai red curry is medium spicy and has a citrus flavor by adding lemongrass, lime peel, and galangal besides other ingredients.

Thai yellow curry is less spicy than the red curry and contains more turmeric that gives it the yellow color

Thai green curry contains cilantro and Jalapenos instead of chili powder

Berbere Mix

Berbere is a spice mix used to make many Ethiopian dishes such as *doro wat* (chicken) and *misir wat* (split lentil). Berbere mix usually consists of chili powder, coriander, nutmeg, allspice, cinnamon, cloves, fenugreek, garlic, ginger, and onion powder.

Curry paste

Curry paste is an alternative to curry powder. Curry paste is made by grinding the curry masala or ingredients into a paste form. Curry masala usually includes fresh ginger instead of ginger powder, fresh garlic and at times tomato puree or paste and shallots or red onions. In some cases, vinegar is added to make it a paste. Most often the curry paste is fried in oil to make sure the spices, onions, tomatoes, and other ingredients are cooked and cured. Frying the curry paste in oil enhances its flavor and also increases its shelf life.

Chapter 2. Ingredients For Curry Powder and Spice Mixes

Turmeric

Required ingredient for curry powder.

Turmeric has been in use over several thousands of years in Asia. Curcumin, an active ingredient in turmeric, has antioxidant, anti-inflammatory and anti-bacterial properties and is a key ingredient in Indian curry powder. For more on turmeric, please see my book titled *"Essential Spices and Herbs: Turmeric"*.

Coriander

Required ingredient for curry powder.

The amount of coriander powder used in the curry blend depends on how mild one wants the curry powder to be. More coriander makes for a milder mix.

Coriander is the seed cultivated from the herb cilantro or Chinese parsley. Coriander seeds have been cultivated for a long time. Coriander has several health benefits including lowering blood sugar, decreasing blood pressure, and lowering cholesterol levels.

Cumin

Required ingredient for curry powder.

Cumin is one of the most widely used spices. Cumin comes in the form of whole dried seeds or ground as a powder and is an integral part of Indian, Mexican, African, South Asian and other cuisines. Like other spices mentioned before, cumin also has a long history. Cumin has many benefits including help with digestion, help with diabetes, anemia, and sleep loss.

Mustard seeds

Mustard seeds are an optional ingredient for curry powder.

Mustard seed is from the mustard plant which is related to broccoli, cabbage, and Brussels sprouts. Three different varieties of mustard seeds are popular: black, brown, and yellow. Mustard seeds are a good source of selenium, magnesium, and omega-3. Mustard seeds have anti-cancer and anti-inflammatory benefits among others.

Fenugreek

Optional ingredient for curry powder.

Fenugreek is a native of the Mediterranean countries and West Asia and is part of the Fabaceae or the bean family. Fenugreek seeds are used as medicine and spice in the middle east, India, and the Mediterranean. Fenugreek is considered to have benefits in treating diabetes, cholesterol, and improve blood sugar levels. Fenugreek is also believed to benefit milk production in breastfeeding, improve digestion, and reduce inflammation.

Fennel

Optional ingredient for curry powder.

Like many other spices we have discussed so far, Fennel was highly valued by ancient civilizations. Fennel belongs to the parsley family which also includes cumin, anise, and dill. Fennel is highly nutritious and has good medicinal value. Fennel is good for indigestion, an upset stomach, flatulence, and bloating. Fennel is also known to help with respiratory problems (such as asthma), boosts the immune system, and treats heartburn.

Lemongrass

Lemongrass is seldom used in South Asian curry recipes but is a required ingredient for Thai curry preparations.

Lemongrass is a tropical herb with a strong citrus flavor and is widely used in Chinese, Thai and Vietnamese cuisine in curries, salads, soups, and sauces. Like some of the other herbs, lemongrass is packed with anti-oxidants and has many other medicinal properties including regulating blood pressure, improving digestion, and boosting metabolism among others.

Lemon peel

Like lemongrass, lemon peel is seldom used in South Asian curry preparations but is often used as an ingredient in Thai curries.

Lemon peel or zest is made by using a sharp knife to make thin slices of lemon peel and then chopping it finely. Lemon peel does contain some vitamins and minerals and compounds that are known to help with cholesterol, cancer and improve bone health.

Curry leaves

Depending on the region in South Asia, curry leaves are used as an optional flavor-enhancing ingredient. Fresh curry leaves are often fried in oil to release their aroma and flavor prior to sautéing onions and curry powder.

Dried curry leaves are ground and added as part of some spice mixes such as sambhar, or rasam powder. One can find curry leaves in Indian and Asian stores in North America and Europe. The benefits of curry leaves include helping with digestion, fighting diabetes, and lowering cholesterol.

Garlic

Optional ingredient in curry preparation.

Garlic is part of the *Allium* (onion) family and is closely related to shallots, onions, Chinese onions, chives, and leeks. There are more than 400 varieties of garlic in the world today.

Garlic is extremely nutritious and is a source of vitamins C and B6, along with minerals such as manganese and selenium. Garlic also contains minor amounts of other minerals such as calcium, copper, potassium, phosphorous, and iron. From a medicinal standpoint, garlic has anti-oxidant, anti-inflammatory, and anti-microbial and anti-viral properties. Garlic is good at reducing cholesterol and blood pressure and also has anti-cancer properties. For more on garlic, please see my book titled *"Essential Spices and Herbs: Garlic"*.

Shallots and onions

Onions and shallots are not usually part of curry powder but are used at times as part of curry paste. However, onions are an integral part of the curry preparation as onions are usually sautéed in oil prior to adding the curry powder.

Foods in the onion family (garlic, red/yellow/white onions, shallots, scallions, chives) all have high anti-oxidant capabilities and contain natural compounds that prevent cell growth. Onions are highly effective cancer fighters and can be found in many of the recipes in this book.

Ginger

Required ingredient for curry powder.

Ginger is widely used in Asian cooking and has been in use for a very long time. Ginger is extremely good for your gut which is the seat of the body's immune system. Like turmeric, ginger has antioxidant and anti-inflammatory properties as well as many other health benefits. For more on ginger, please see my book titled *"Essential Spices and Herbs: Ginger"*.

Cinnamon

Required ingredient for most curry powder blends.

Cinnamon is also a spice used for thousands of years and is well known for its fragrance and sweetness. Used primarily in baking, cinnamon is one of the healthiest spices on earth. Cinnamon is packed with antioxidants, anti-inflammatory, anti-bacterial, and anti-fungal agents. Cinnamon is good in fighting common infections due to its anti-microbial properties. Other benefits include lower and more stabilized blood sugar levels in diabetes patients, lower cholesterol, and improved brain function. For more on cinnamon, please see my book titled *"Essential Spices and Herbs: Cinnamon"*.

Clove

Required ingredient for most curry powder blends.

Cloves are the aromatic flower buds of an evergreen tree native of South Asia. Used extensively in Indian cuisine, clove has a history of centuries of use. Clove boosts the immune system, helps with digestion and has many other benefits

Chili Peppers and Chili Powder

Chili powder is a required ingredient for curry powder.

How much of chili powder and the kind of chili (mildest to hottest) used in the curry powder mix depends on one's "heat" tolerance of the curry spice mix.

The active ingredient contained in chili pepper is called capsaicin which gives the pungent or hot taste. Chili pepper contains anti-oxidants, vitamin C, and carotenoids that provide a number of health benefits including boosting immunity, better cardiovascular health, clearing nasal and chest congestion, losing weight, and treating diabetes. Chili pepper is a key component of Indian curry powder as well as many Mexican and Asian cuisine.

Cardamom

Required ingredient for most curry powder blends.

Cardamom is a spice that originated in the Indian subcontinent and is part of the ginger family. Like many other spices, cardamom is loaded with nutrients and other helpful agents that offer many health benefits from curing common colds to indigestion, lower blood pressure, improved circulation, heartburn, constipation, and many more. Cardamom is used in baking and in South Asian cooking. Cardamom has a distinct taste that I like. I always put one or two cardamom pods in my black or milk tea to enhance flavor. I also add cardamom when I make rice dishes – both savory and sweet.

Black Pepper

Required ingredient for most curry powder blends.

Black pepper is originally from Southern India but is currently cultivated in Vietnam, Brazil, India, and other tropical countries. Black pepper has many amazing benefits including preventing cancer, relieving colds and coughs, improving digestion, and many other benefits. Black pepper is also known for enhancing bioavailability whereby, it enhances the absorption of nutrients in other foods we consume. For example, adding black pepper to turmeric helps curcumin absorption by 1000 times.

Allspice

Usually not part of Indian curry powder but used in other blends such as Ethiopian berbere and Japanese curry paste.

Allspice is the dried unripe fruit of an evergreen tree or shrub *Pimenta dioica*. Allspice was originated in the West Indies and was primarily cultivated in Jamaica. The dried fruit is spice and is considered to have a combined flavor of many spices, especially cinnamon, nutmeg, and cloves, and hence it was called allspice by the English. Allspice is a key ingredient in Caribbean cuisine. Like many other spices, allspice's benefits include improving circulation, aid in digestion, and improving heart health. Allspice also has both anti-inflammatory and anti-oxidant properties.

Chapter 3. Curry Powder And Spice Mix Recipes

Recipe #1: Quick and Easy Mild Curry Powder

Ingredients:

- 2 tablespoons of ground cumin
- 3 tablespoons of ground coriander
- 2 tablespoons ground turmeric
- ½ tablespoon ground ginger
- ½ tablespoon ground chili powder

Method

Put all the ingredients in a glass jar. Close with a lid. Mix it well and the curry powder is ready! Use a 1-2 teaspoon at a time or as required and store the rest in a cool, dry place.

This is the simplest and quickest way to make curry powder. Since the chili powder is much less by proportion, this curry powder is a mild version. By adjusting the chili powder proportion or by selecting different varieties (from mild to hot) chili powder, one can change the level of "heat" with this blend.

Recipe #2: Spicy Curry Powder

Ingredients:

- 4 tablespoons of ground coriander
- 2 tablespoons ground turmeric
- 2 tablespoons of ground cumin or 1-1 1/2 tablespoons cumin seeds
- ½ tablespoon ground ginger
- ½ tablespoon whole black peppercorns
- 6 cardamom whole pods
- 6 whole cloves
- ½ inch cinnamon stick
- 1 tablespoon ground ginger
- ½ - 1 tablespoon red chili flakes
- 1 tablespoon paprika (optional)

Method

Put all the ingredients in a spice blender and blend for 2 minutes, or until the spice mix is ground to a fine powder.

Transfer into an airtight container and store in a cool, dry place. Use 1-2 teaspoons (or more depending on your tolerance level) while sautéing vegetables, meat, etc.

RECIPE #3: MILD CURRY POWDER

By increasing the proportion of coriander, cumin, and turmeric to that of chili, one can create mild curry powder.

Ingredients:

- 2 tablespoons of ground coriander
- 2 tablespoons ground turmeric
- 2 tablespoons of ground cumin
- ½ tablespoons ground ginger
- ½ inch cinnamon stick
- ½ - 1 tablespoon red chili flakes
- ½ tablespoon mustard seeds
- ½ tsp ground cardamom or 3 whole cardamom

Method

Put all the ingredients in a spice blender and blend for 2 minutes, or until the spice mix is ground to a fine powder.

Transfer into an airtight container and store in a cool, dry place. Use 1-2 teaspoons (or more depending on your tolerance level) while sautéing vegetables, meat, etc.

RECIPE #4: VERY MILD RED CURRY POWDER

This is one of the mildest curry powder blends as chili powder is replaced by paprika. Paprika also adds a nice red color and a light sweet taste.

Ingredients:

- 3 tablespoons of ground paprika
- 2 tablespoons ground turmeric
- 2 tablespoons of ground cumin
- 2 tablespoons of ground coriander
- 2 tablespoons of ground fennel
- 1 tablespoon ground ginger
- 2 tablespoon ground brown or yellow mustard
- ½ tablespoon ground cardamom
- ½ inch cinnamon stick or ½ tablespoon ground cinnamon
- 6 whole cloves or ½ tablespoon ground cloves

Method

Put all the ingredients in a spice blender and blend for 2 minutes, or until the spice mix ground to a fine powder.

Transfer into an airtight container and store in a cool, dry place. Use 1-2 teaspoons (or more depending on your tolerance level) while sautéing vegetables, meat, etc.

CURRY: Curry Powder and Spice Mixes

RECIPE #5: BASIC THAI RED CURRY PASTE

The next three recipes are for Thai curry pastes.

Ingredients:

- 2 teaspoons coriander or coriander powder
- 1 teaspoon cumin seeds or cumin powder
- ½-inch fresh ginger peeled
- ½ tablespoon whole black peppercorns
- 1 teaspoon grated galangal (if available)
- 1 teaspoon lime zest
- 1 stalk lemongrass chopped
- 1 tablespoon chopped cilantro (stems and roots included, if available)
- 1 teaspoon kaffir lime rind chopped, or 4 kaffir lime leaves torn into pieces (if available)
- 10 large red chilies – medium-hot variety, chopped after soaking in warm water for ½ hour
- 2 teaspoons of shrimp paste or Thai fish sauce
- 1/8 cup red onion chopped, or 2-3 shallots chopped
- 4 garlic cloves peeled and chopped
- ¼ cup water used to soak the chilies

Method

1. If using whole seeds, dry roast cumin, coriander, and peppercorns for 2 minutes on medium heat. Let it cool down. If powders are used, go directly to step 2.
2. Put all the ingredients in a spice blender and add water. Blend for 2-3 minutes or until the spice blended into a fine paste.

Transfer into an airtight container and store in the fridge. Use 1-2 teaspoons (or more depending on your tolerance level) for delicious Thai red curry. Recipes follow later in the book.

CURRY: Curry Powder and Spice Mixes

RECIPE #6: THAI GREEN CURRY PASTE

Ingredients:

- 4-6 medium jalapeños, sliced with seeds removed
- ¼ cup red onions, chopped (or 4-6 shallots, sliced)
- 2-inch fresh ginger peeled and chopped
- 4 garlic cloves
- 1 bunch fresh cilantro, including stems and roots (if available) chopped
- 2 lemongrass stalks chopped
- Lime juice, 1 full lime
- 8 kaffir lime leaves, torn into pieces (if available)
- Zest from 1 lime
- 1 inch piece galangal, peeled and chopped (if available)
- 2 teaspoons coriander powder or coriander seeds
- 1 teaspoon cumin powder or cumin seeds
- 1 teaspoon whole black peppercorns
- 2 teaspoons Thai fish sauce or shrimp paste, or light soy sauce
- 1/8 cup of warm water

Method

1. If using whole seeds, dry roast cumin, coriander, and peppercorns for 2 minutes on medium heat. Let it cool down. If powders are used, go directly to step 2.
2. Put all the ingredients in a spice blender and add water. Blend for 2-3 minutes or until the spice blended into a fine paste.

Transfer into an airtight container and store in the fridge. Use 1-2 teaspoons (or more depending on your tolerance level) for delicious Thai red curry. Recipes follow later in the book.

RECIPE #7: THAI YELLOW CURRY PASTE

Ingredients:

- ¼ cup red onions, chopped
- 2-inch fresh ginger peeled and chopped
- 4 garlic cloves
- 1 bunch fresh cilantro, including stems and roots (if available) chopped
- 2 lemongrass stalks chopped
- Lime juice, 1 full lime
- 1 teaspoon mild curry powder
- 1 teaspoon turmeric powder
- 2-4 Thai red chilies
- 2 tsp Thai fish sauce, or shrimp paste or light soy sauce

Method

1. Put all the ingredients in a spice blender and add water. Blend for 2-3 minutes or until the spice blended into a fine paste.

Transfer into an airtight container and store in the fridge. Use 1-2 teaspoons (or more depending on your tolerance level) for delicious Thai red curry. Recipes follow later in the book.

RECIPE #8: INDIAN CURRY PASTE

Ingredients:

Ingredients to create a paste

CURRY: Curry Powder and Spice Mixes

- 1 cup red onions or shallots chopped
- 1 teaspoon cumin seeds or cumin powder
- 1-inch fresh ginger peeled and sliced
- 4 garlic cloves peeled
- 1 jalapeno or green chili – seeds out
- 1/8 cup water

Whole spices for roasting and making spice powder:
- 1 teaspoon whole black ground peppercorns
- 1 teaspoon whole cloves
- 3 teaspoons coriander seeds
- 4-6 whole cardamom pods or 2 black cardamom pods
- 1 teaspoon cumin seeds
- 2 bay leaves
- 1-1 ½ teaspoons turmeric powder
- ½-1 teaspoon chili powder (mild, medium or hot depending on your tolerance level)
- 2 tablespoons coconut or vegetable oil
- 1 cup fresh tomatoes pureed

Method
1. Grind the first set of ingredients in a blender to create a paste and set aside.
2. Roast all the whole spices in a pan on medium heat for about 2 minutes. Let it cool and then grind them together in a spice grinder and make a spice mix.
3. Heat oil in a pan and add the paste and cook it for 3-5 minutes mixing well on medium heat.
4. Now add the spices mix, turmeric, and salt mix well. Mix well to make sure the spices get cooked and also does not stick to the bottom. This will take 2-3 minutes.

5. Now add the pureed tomatoes and cook until the water evaporates, and tomato is cooked. Mix well.
6. Switch off the heat and let it cool down.

Transfer into an airtight container and store in the fridge.

RECIPE #9: GARAM MASALA

Ingredients:

- 4 tablespoons of ground coriander
- 2 tablespoons ground turmeric
- 2 tablespoons of ground cumin or 1-1 1/2 tablespoon(s) cumin seeds
- 1/2 tablespoons ground ginger
- 1/2 tablespoon whole black peppercorns
- 6 cardamom whole pods
- 6 whole cloves
- ½ inch cinnamon stick
- 1 tablespoon ground ginger
- ½ - 1 tablespoon red chili flakes
- 1 tablespoon paprika (optional)

Method

Put all the ingredients in a spice blender and blend for 2 minutes, or until the spice mix ground to a fine powder.

Transfer into an airtight container and store in a cool, dry place. Use 1-2 teaspoons (or more depending on your tolerance level) while sautéing vegetables, meat, etc.

RECIPE #10: ETHIOPIAN BERBERE MIX

Recipe adapted from epicurious.com. Berbere is readily available to buy from online retailers such as Amazon.

Ingredients:

- ½ tsp ground fenugreek
- ½ cup mild chili powder such as hatch chili pepper or Anaheim chili peppers
- ¼ cup paprika powder
- ½ tablespoon ground ginger
- ½ tablespoon ground onion
- ½ tablespoon ground garlic
- 1 teaspoon ground cumin
- 1 teaspoon ground allspice
- ¼ teaspoon ground nutmeg
- ½ teaspoon ground cardamom
- 1/8 teaspoon ground cinnamon
- 1/8 teaspoon ground cloves

Method

Mix all the ingredients together. If using any of the spices in seeds form, use a spice grinder to grind them first, and then mix them together.

Transfer into an airtight container and store in a cool, dry place.

RECIPE #11: JAMAICAN CURRY POWDER

Ingredients:

- 1 tablespoon ground fenugreek or whole seeds

CURRY: Curry Powder and Spice Mixes

- 2 tablespoons of ground or whole cumin seeds
- 1 tablespoon ground allspice/ whole seeds
- 2 tablespoons of ground anise or anise seeds
- 4-5 tablespoons of ground turmeric
- 4 tablespoons of ground coriander (or coriander seeds)
- 2 tablespoons of ground or whole mustard seeds

Method

If powders are used, combine all the powders into a glass jar and mix well.

If whole seeds are used, combine all the whole seeds and roast them in a skillet on medium heat and then grind them in a spice grinder.

Transfer into an airtight container and store in a cool, dry place.

OTHER SPICE BLENDS

Taco seasoning spice blend

Ingredients

- 4 tablespoons chili powder (mild/medium/hot) depending on the heat level
- 2 tablespoons cumin powder
- 2 teaspoons garlic powder
- 3 teaspoons onion powder
  1 teaspoon oregano
- 1 teaspoon black pepper powder
- 2 teaspoons paprika
- 1 teaspoon salt or to taste
  1 teaspoon turmeric (optional)
- 1 teaspoon ginger powder (optional)

Put all the ingredients in a glass jar and shake well. Keep it in a cool dry place.

Cajun seasoning spice blend

Ingredients

- 4 tablespoons paprika
- 1 tablespoon black pepper powder
- 2 tablespoons garlic powder
- 1 tablespoon onion powder
- 1 tablespoon oregano
- 1 teaspoon cayenne powder
- 1 teaspoon salt or to taste

- 2 teaspoons of thyme

Put all the ingredients in a glass jar and shake well. Keep it in a cool dry place.

Fajita seasoning spice blend

Ingredients

- 1 tablespoon paprika
- 2 tablespoons chili powder
- 2 teaspoons garlic powder
- 1 teaspoon onion powder
- 2 tablespoons cumin powder
- 1 teaspoon salt or to taste

Put all the ingredients in a glass jar and shake well. Keep it in a cool dry place.

Chapter 4. Health Benefits Of Curry Powder

Many of the ingredients used in curry powder have been in use for centuries for their medicinal properties. Below are some of the benefits of curry powder

Reducing Inflammation

Anti-inflammatory properties of curry powder come from turmeric, ginger, and cinnamon.

Inflammation plays an important role in the natural healing process in the human body. It helps to defend harmful invaders in our body such as bacteria that cause infection. Inflammation also helps the body carry out wound repair. Without inflammation, these foreign invaders could cause damage to our bodies and ultimately kill us.

While short term, controlled inflammation is beneficial, it can become a major problem when it becomes chronic, such as arthritis. Chronic inflammation plays a major role in many serious health conditions such as heart disease, cancer, Alzheimer's, and other various degenerative conditions.

Therefore, it is very important that inflammation is contained, and chronic inflammation condition is fought with either medicines, supplements, through foods, or through a combination of both in order to reduce or prevent it from happening.

The key ingredients in curry powder that helps reduce inflammation are turmeric, ginger, cinnamon, and coriander.

Curcumin, the main active ingredient in Turmeric, has high anti-inflammatory properties so much so that it can be as effective as some of the prescription anti-inflammatory drugs without any side effects.

Ginger has been used for centuries as an anti-inflammatory herb. Recent studies have shown that a steady intake of ginger for a period of more than a month helped reduce inflammation in the colon. By reducing inflammation, the risk of colon cancer is also reduced. Another study has shown promise in reducing inflammation associated with osteoarthritis.

Cinnamon's highly effective anti-oxidant compounds also exhibit anti-inflammatory properties. Many flavonoid compounds in cinnamon have been identified as effective against systemic inflammation throughout the body. These properties in cinnamon protect against cancer, heart diseases, neurological degeneration, and many other health issues.

While not usually a part of curry powder, fresh garlic is used in the preparation of curry. Allicin, the sulfur compound in garlic, has high anti-inflammatory properties that stimulate the body's defenses and disease-fighting capabilities and helps fight inflammation effectively.

Antioxidant Properties

CURRY: Curry Powder and Spice Mixes

Many of the ingredients in curry powder have anti-oxidant properties including turmeric, cinnamon, cloves, chili powder, and ginger.

Oxidative damage caused by free radicals (highly reactive molecules with unpaired electrons) contributes to the risk of cancers, heart disease, and diabetes as well as age-related macular degeneration. Free radicals tend to react with important organic substances, such as fatty acids, proteins, or DNA, causing oxidative damage.

Antioxidants help neutralize free radicals and reduce the risk of oxidative damage. They "clean up" free radicals by interacting and forming harmless substances, thereby protecting healthy cells. There are several vitamins and supplements that are known to have antioxidant properties, such as, vitamins C and E and beta carotene. Many of the fruits (berries, grapes, etc.) and vegetables (kale, artichokes, bell pepper, etc.) contain antioxidants. Nuts such as walnuts and beverages such as tea and coffee also contain antioxidants. Antioxidants are often added to packaged food products to keep them from interacting with air.

Many spices included in the curry blend is known to have significant antioxidant properties. These include turmeric, ginger, cinnamon, cloves, and others. However, cinnamon is known to have one of the highest anti-oxidants among the many commonly used foods. In a study of 26 common spices and herbs on their anti-oxidant properties, cinnamon came out on top eclipsing garlic, oregano, thyme, cloves, and many other spices.

The active ingredient in turmeric is a potent antioxidant that can do two things: neutralize free radicals due to its chemical structure and stimulate the body's own antioxidant enzymes.

FIGHTING CANCER

Cancer-fighting properties of curry powder come from the ingredients turmeric, ginger, chili, and cinnamon.

There have been studies conducted on the effects of ginger in colorectal cancer patients that have shown the effectiveness of ginger in arresting the growth of cancer cells. This may not be surprising given how good ginger for the gastrointestinal system. Ginger is believed to be also effective in other forms of cancer such as pancreatic cancer, ovarian cancer, and breast cancer. Further studies are required to confirm these.

As like many other spices and herbs, cinnamon's anti-oxidant, anti-inflammatory, and anti-viral/microbial properties result in it is also effective against cancer.

Cinnamaldehyde compound present in cinnamon has the capability to inhibit tumor growth and protect cell damage. Cinnamon can help improve the health of the colon and protect against colon cancer as shown in some of the studies.

There have been several studies conducted on the effects of turmeric on cancer cells. These tests in the lab have shown that turmeric can kill or arrest the growth of cancer cells. Some studies on test animals have shown that turmeric blocked the formation of cancer-causing enzymes. Thus, turmeric, not only could be used as a treatment but as a prevention as well.

Turmeric as part of a regular diet keeps your digestive system healthy and helps ward off colon cancer.

According to the American Association for Cancer Research, **capsaicin**, the active ingredient in chili powder has shown to kill leukemia and cancer cells. Similar to turmeric, chilies can also inhibit cell growth preventing or arresting tumor and cancer progression.

Fighting Alzheimer's Disease

Alzheimer's fighting properties of curry powder come from two key ingredients in curry powder: turmeric and cinnamon.

Alzheimer's is a form of dementia characterized by progressive loss of cognitive function. Alzheimer's is the most common form of dementia and about 6 million people in the US and close to 50 million people worldwide live with Alzheimer's.

Cinnamon's antioxidant and anti-inflammatory properties work well reducing the oxidative damage to the brain cells as well as inflammation helping to slow down the disease progression and possibly delay the onset.

Cinnamaldehyde and epicatechin, two of the active compounds found in cinnamon have been studied on their effects of tau proteins that cause tangles in Alzheimer's brain. Researchers have found some evidence that these compounds in cinnamon can prevent the formation of tangles thus likely preventing or delaying Alzheimer's.

Diabetes and Alzheimer's are known to share connections similar to a heart condition and Alzheimer's. 70% of people with type 2 diabetes are known to eventually develop Alzheimer's. So, cinnamon's ability to regulate insulin levels and thus help control diabetes may also have an indirect benefit by reducing the risk of Alzheimer's.

Though it has not been conclusively proven, there is some anecdotal evidence that **curcumin in turmeric** could prevent the formation or even break up of amyloid-beta plaques considered to be associated with Alzheimer's disease.

Another compound in turmeric called **turmerone** has shown in some studies to help create new brain cells by stimulating stem cells. This could help with arresting neurodegenerative conditions and help reduce the mental decline as people age.

PARKINSON'S

Cinnamon is the key ingredient that helps fight Parkinson's.

Parkinson's disease (PD) is a neurological disorder that continues to deteriorate over time and impact a person's ability to control and regulate their movements. There are about 10 million PD patients worldwide with about 100,000 being diagnosed every year in the US alone and about 10,000 in the UK.

As PD progresses, less and less dopamine is produced. Dopamine is a chemical that helps transmit messages (neurotransmitters) to nerve cells (neurons) that control movements. As a result, a person's ability to regulate and control movements are impacted more and more.

Some studies have shown that regular intake of cinnamon helps prevent the loss of neuroprotective proteins (Parkin and D-J1) that protects brain cells.

A study by the researches at Rush University Medical Center found that cinnamon can reverse the changes that occur in the brain as a result of Parkinson's. The study was conducted in mice. The study found that cinnamon is metabolized in the liver into sodium benzoate which then enters the brain and can prevent the loss of Parkin and DJ-1 proteins that protect brain cells.

Lower Blood Pressure

Elevated blood pressure or hypertension is one of the key contributors to heart diseases such as heart attacks and strokes.

A number of studies in humans have found that the daily intake of garlic has very beneficial effects in lowering hypertension. In some studies, these benefits were as good as some of the prescription medications.

Neuro-protective

Besides Alzheimer's and Parkinson's diseases, cinnamon provides protection against neuro-degeneration as part of normal aging as well. Since cinnamon contains a high level of anti-oxidants and has high anti-inflammatory properties, cinnamons help prevents oxidative damage to brain cells as well as lower inflammation in the brain. As a result, cinnamon acts as a protective agent to brain cells resulting in slowing down cognitive decline due to aging.

Ginger has antioxidant and anti-inflammatory properties that can help with slowing down the age-related decline in brain functions such as Alzheimer's diseases.

Turmeric also is known for its neuroprotective properties.

DIABETES AND HEART HEALTH

Ginger is believed to have several properties that help in maintaining a healthy heart including blood thinning, stimulating circulation, reducing cholesterol levels, and preventing heart attacks and strokes.

A study conducted on gingerol effect on blood sugar found that there were significant benefits of using ginger powder in lowering blood sugar levels in diabetic patients.

One of the active ingredients in cinnamon, *hydroxychalcone* is believed to help increase insulin sensitivity and help promote insulin uptake into the cells.

One of the flavonoids found in cinnamon called proanthocyanins, is considered to penetrate cells and help in maintaining insulin balance within the cells.

Cinnamon is known to have a positive influence on the digestive enzymes in the stomach. Cinnamon helps in slowing down the breakdown of carbohydrates and thus regulate post-meal insulin levels.

These are all extremely beneficial properties of cinnamon in countering diabetic conditions. Numerous studies have confirmed the anti-diabetic effects of cinnamon.

Besides cinnamon, both cumin and coriander seeds have shown evidence of effectiveness in regulating blood sugar and thus helping in preventing or slowing diabetes.

CHOLESTEROL

Several ingredients in curry powder can help lower cholesterol levels such as turmeric, fenugreek, ginger, and garlic (used as part of curry preparation).

Studies have shown that a daily intake of ginger helps reduce LDL cholesterol (bad cholesterol). The studies were conducted in humans as well as animals. As a result, the daily use of ginger may help maintain not only a healthy gut but a healthy heart as well.

Studies have shown that daily intake of cinnamon may help reduce LDL cholesterol (bad cholesterol) and likely improve HDL cholesterol. While there is no conclusive evidence in organized studies about the benefits of cinnamon in lowering cholesterol, several anecdotal evidence and claims exist regarding the cholesterol-lowering abilities of cinnamon.

Research has shown that feeding lab animals with turmeric extract resulted in reducing bad cholesterol and increasing good cholesterol, thereby reducing total cholesterol levels. In most studies, the improvements were in the 25-50% range. Curcumin's antioxidant property helps prevent oxidation of cholesterol, helps increase the metabolism of cholesterol, and reduces build-up.

Garlic is believed to reduce both LDL (bad cholesterol), and total cholesterol. A number of research studies in humans and animals have found that the sulfur compounds in garlic help reduce LDL cholesterol and total cholesterol while they have no impact on HDL (good cholesterol) levels.

Fenugreek has been proven to lower both cholesterol and blood sugar levels.

INDIGESTION, BLOATING, CONSTIPATION, IBS

Curry powder has several ingredients that are very useful for the digestive system. Ginger, fennel, cumin, coriander, turmeric, and fenugreek – all of them are known to help with digestion, prevent bloating, and keep the digestive system healthy.

Ginger has been used in traditional medicine as a digestive aid for thousands of years. In the East, ginger is an essential ingredient in meat cooking not only to add flavor to the food but also to help with digestion as well. Chewing on fresh ginger or drinking ginger juice/drink can help cure minor tummy aches (due to indigestion) and help with bloating and constipation.

Ginger relieves and relaxes gastrointestinal muscles that help reduce stomach irritation. It also helps in bile production and movement of food through the gastrointestinal tract and thereby helping proper metabolism and food absorption in the body.

Fennel and Cumin help with indigestion, bloating, constipation and Irritable Bowel Syndrome (IBS). Curry powder has a good amount of ginger, cumin, and fennel (in some blends).

Studies have shown several benefits for turmeric in gastrointestinal problems. Turmeric stimulates the gallbladder in order to produce more bile, which helps in digestion and promotes intestinal flora. Due to its anti-inflammatory properties, several inflammatory bowel diseases such as Chron's and Ulcerative Colitis could benefit from turmeric intake. The usage of turmeric helps to heal the digestive system and supports the growth of good bacteria.

Immune System & Infections

Most of the ingredients in curry powder have anti-bacterial, antiviral, anti-fungal, and anti-microbial properties. During the middle ages, spices like turmeric, chili powder, and cinnamon were used as a food preservative due to these properties. Coriander is considered effective in treating foodborne diseases such as salmonella. All these spices have properties that make them a good choice for fighting various infections. Infections as simple as a common cold to infections such as lung and other respiratory tract infections caused by bacteria or fungi can be fought with warm curry soup.

As ginger has anti-oxidant, anti-inflammatory, and anti-microbial properties, its use helps in an improved immune system. Studies have shown that ginger extract can prevent growth or even kill some of the bacteria and viruses. Studies have been conducted on the effects of gingerol against bacteria that cause gingivitis and periodontitis that have shown ginger to be effective against these. Another study has

CURRY: Curry Powder and Spice Mixes

shown that fresh ginger is effective against respiratory infections. Studies have shown that ginger is also effective against fungal infections.

Curry made with curry powder, fresh ginger, garlic, and other herbs provide additional benefits in fighting bacteria and infections. Allicin, the sulfur compound found in garlic has anti-microbial, anti-fungal and anti-virus capabilities. A bowl of warm mild curry soup can be effective in 1. Preventing a cold and flu and 2. Speedy recovery in cases where the subjects of the study did catch a cold.

This is one of the reasons garlic was used as a remedy for plague and smallpox during medieval times.

PAIN AND ARTHRITIS

Arthritis is a common health condition characterized by inflammation of joints. Due to its powerful anti-inflammatory characteristics, it is not surprising that turmeric can be effective in treating various kinds of arthritis. Several studies have shown that turmeric is effective in reducing pain, joint inflammation, and discomfort in rheumatoid arthritis (RA) one of the most common autoimmune diseases. Curcumin in turmeric is known to block inflammatory cytokines and enzymes. Some recent studies have shown that turmeric is effective in preventing RA as well as providing long term benefits, and some anecdotal reports have indicated that curcumin extract has found to be highly effective in dogs with arthritis.

With its anti-inflammatory and antioxidant properties, it is no wonder that, turmeric is an effective remedy for pain;

especially joint pains as a result of inflammation or arthritis. Some studies in rats have shown that turmeric naturally activates the body's inherent pain-relieving mechanisms.

Besides turmeric, chili pepper is also studied for pain-relieving properties.

IMPROVED CIRCULATION

Studies have shown that curcumin has properties that help in unclogging your arteries and improving blood circulation. Turmeric could be considered a natural alternative to some of the common medications that help prevent blood clotting. A recent study in Japan showed that curcumin-improved blood circulation in a trial group did the same as a group that did regular exercise. Improving circulation also helps with improved brain function and fighting age-related decline in brain cells.

Chapter 5. Cooking With Curry Powder And Spice Mixes

Bell Pepper And Chicken Stir Fry

Ingredients

- 1 bell pepper washed and cut into thin slices
- 2 teaspoons coconut oil (olive oil or vegetable oil can be used as well)
- 2 lb. boneless chicken breast cut into 1-inch pieces
- 1 teaspoon turmeric powder
- 1 teaspoon black pepper powder
- 1 teaspoon coriander powder
- 1 medium onion sliced
- ½ inch piece of ginger, thinly sliced
- 1 medium tomato chopped
- 3 cloves of garlic chopped
- 1 Jalapeño pepper sliced into thin pieces (optional)
- ¼ cup cilantro chopped (optional)

Method

1. Sprinkle ½ teaspoon of turmeric powder, pepper powder, and salt on the washed and cut chicken. Mix well and set aside for 10 minutes.
2. In a pan, heat oil, add onions, crushed garlic, ginger, and optional Jalapeno. Sauté until onions become translucent.
3. Add the rest of the turmeric powder, coriander powder, and pepper powder and mix well.
4. Add the chopped tomato and mix.
5. Now add the bell pepper and chicken and mix well.

6. Cover and cook for 10 minutes on medium heat or until chicken and peppers are cooked. Stir occasionally.
7. Switch off the heat, add optional cilantro, add salt to taste.

Serve with rice or bread.

Coconut Curry Chicken

Basic Ingredients

- 2 lbs. chicken breast cut into small (1 inch) pieces
- 1-2 teaspoons of curry powder, depending on your tolerance on spice
- 1 teaspoon turmeric
- 1 medium onion, chopped
- 2-3 teaspoons oil
- ½ teaspoon pepper powder
- 2 medium potatoes – peeled and cut into 1-inch cubes
- 3-4 cloves of garlic, crushed
- ½ inch cube of ginger, peeled and chopped
- 1 can (14 oz) of coconut milk
- ¼ cup mint leaves or cilantro
- ½ -1 can of chicken broth (depending on the amount gravy desired)

Optional Ingredients

- 1 cup sliced carrots
- 2 medium chopped tomatoes

Method

1. Sprinkle 1 tsp curry powder, ½ teaspoon turmeric, and ¼ tsp salt on cut chicken. Mix well and keep it aside for 10 minutes
2. In a separate pan, heat oil, sauté onions, garlic, and ginger until onions become translucent.
3. Add remaining curry powder, turmeric, and pepper powder. Mix for 1-2 minutes.
4. Add the chicken and potato and the optional tomato and carrots. Mix well for 1-2 minutes until the chicken and potato are coated with the gravy.
5. Add chicken broth and bring it to a boil. Stir well.
6. Reduce heat to low medium, cover the pan and cook for 10-12 minutes or until chicken, potatoes and carrots are well mixed and chicken loses its pink color and the potatoes and carrots are about half cooked.
7. Add the coconut milk, cover, and simmer on low heat for another 20 minutes or until chicken, potatoes, and carrots are cooked well and are soft.
8. Add mint leaves/cilantro and stir. Add salt to taste. Switch off the heat and keep it covered for 1-2 minutes before serving.

Serve with rice or bread.

BEEF/CHICKEN PEPPER FRY

Ingredients

- 2 lbs. boneless chicken breast/beef cut into 1-inch cubes/stripes
- 2 teaspoons coconut oil (olive oil or vegetable oil can be used as well)
- 1 teaspoon black pepper powder
- 2 teaspoons curry powder
- 2 large onions sliced
- 2-inch pieces of ginger thinly sliced
- 2-3 medium tomatoes sliced
- 4-6 cloves of garlic crushed
- Cilantro – 1 cup (optional)

Method

1. Heat oil in a medium non-stick pan; add onions, garlic, and ginger. Stir until golden.
2. Add curry powder and pepper powder, stir for 2-3 minutes.
3. Add tomato and mix well.
4. Add chicken and mix so that chicken is coated well with spices and onion.
5. Cover and simmer for 20-25 minutes or until the chicken is cooked stirring occasionally so the chicken or the gravy does not stick to the pan.
6. Garnish with cilantro. Serve with rice or naan (Indian bread).

CURRY: Curry Powder and Spice Mixes

CAULIFLOWER AND POTATO CURRY

Basic Ingredients

- 2 medium potatoes peeled and cut into 1-inch cubes
- ½ head of cauliflower washed and cut into small pieces (same size as the potatoes)
- 2 teaspoon oil
- 1 medium onion sliced
- 1 teaspoon curry powder
- 1-2 medium tomatoes chopped
- ½ teaspoon salt (or to taste)
- ¼ cup fresh cilantro chopped
- ½ cup vegetable broth

Optional Ingredients

- 1-2 jalapenos sliced (seeds out/in)
- 2-3 cloves of garlic crushed
- ½ inch ginger root chopped into fine pieces

Method

1. Heat oil in a medium non-stick pan and crackle optional cumin seeds.
2. Add onions, and optional garlic, ginger, and jalapenos. Stir until onion becomes translucent.
3. Add turmeric, black pepper, and optional curry powder, stir for 1-2 minutes.
4. Add chopped tomatoes, potatoes, and cauliflower, mix well and then add vegetable broth and mix
5. Bring to a boil
6. Cover and simmer for 10-15 minutes, or until the potatoes and cauliflower are cooked.
7. Switch off the heat and add the cilantro and salt.

CURRY: Curry Powder and Spice Mixes

Mix well and serve hot as a side dish with rice or bread.

Recipe Notes

1. There are many optional ingredients listed, one could use all of them or pick and choose based on your taste.
2. The jalapenos vary in their heat level. If you choose to use them, you can take the seeds out to reduce the heat. This note applies to all the recipes in this book.

POTATO CURRY

Basic Ingredients

- 4 medium potatoes, washed
- 2 tsp coconut or olive oil
- 1 medium onion sliced
- 1 tsp turmeric powder
- ½ tsp mild curry powder
- 1-2 medium tomatoes chopped
- ½ tsp salt (or to taste)
- ¼ cup fresh cilantro chopped
- ½ cup vegetable broth

Optional Ingredients
- 1-2 jalapenos sliced (seeds out/in)
- 2-3 cloves of garlic crushed
- ½ inch ginger root chopped into fine pieces or paste
- ½ tsp optional cumin seeds

CURRY: Curry Powder and Spice Mixes

- 1 tbsp bacon powder or fresh bacon pieces
- 1 bell pepper - chopped

Method

1. Boil potatoes, peel and dice them into small pieces and set aside.
2. Heat oil in a medium non-stick pan and crackle optional cumin seeds.
3. Add onions, and optional garlic, ginger and jalapenos. Stir until onion becomes translucent.
4. Add turmeric, stir for 2 minutes.
5. Add chopped tomatoes, optional bell pepper, and boiled and cut potatoes. Mix well and then add vegetable broth.
6. Bring to a boil stirring in between.
7. Cover and simmer for 10-15 minutes, or until the tomatoes are cooked and the potatoes are mashed to the desired level. Stir to make sure potatoes don't stick to the bottom.
8. Switch off the heat, add the cilantro, optional bacon pieces, and salt.

Mix well and serve hot as a side dish with rice or bread.

QUICK FISH CURRY WITH CANNED TUNA

Basic Ingredients

- 3-4 canned chunk light tuna
- 2 tsp coconut or olive oil

CURRY: Curry Powder and Spice Mixes

- 1 medium onion sliced
- 1 tsp turmeric powder
- ½ pepper powder
- 1-2 medium tomatoes chopped
- ½ tsp salt (or to taste)
- ¼ cup fresh cilantro chopped
- ½ cup vegetable broth

Optional Ingredients
- 1-2 jalapenos sliced (seeds out/in)
- 2-3 cloves of garlic crushed
- ½ inch ginger root chopped into fine pieces or paste
- ¼ cup grated coconut

Method

1. Heat oil in a medium non-stick pan, add onions, and optional garlic, ginger, and jalapenos. Stir until onion becomes translucent.
2. Add turmeric and pepper stir for 2 minutes.
3. Add chopped tomatoes, mix well and cook for 3-4 minutes.
4. Add tuna. Cover and simmer for 10-15 minutes, or until the tomatoes are cooked.
5. Switch off heat, add the cilantro and coconut.

Mix well and serve hot as a side dish with rice or bread.

Note 1: There are many optional ingredients listed, one could use all of them or pick and choose based on your taste.

Note 2: The jalapenos vary in their heat level. If you choose to use them, you can take the seeds out to reduce the heat. This note applies to all the recipes in this book.

BELL PEPPER CURRY

Basic Ingredients

- 4 green bell peppers
- ½ cup raw peanuts (or cashews)
- 1 tablespoon coconut oil or olive oil
- 2 medium red onions, chopped
- ½ -1 tsp curry powder
- ¼ cup cilantro

Method

1. Heat ½ tablespoon oil in a medium non-stick pan. Fry peanuts (or cashews) and ½ of the chopped onions and then grind it into a paste.
2. In the same pan, add remaining oil and fry onions. When onions become translucent, add the curry powder and sauté it.
3. Add the bell pepper and salt. Mix it well so that the bell pepper pieces are coated with the curry powder. Cover and cook on low heat for 15 minutes. If needed, stir occasionally so it does not stick to the pan
4. Add the ground peanut/cashew and mix well. Cover and cook for another 5 minutes. Add cilantro and serve.

Mix well and serve hot as a side dish with rice or bread.

CURRY: Curry Powder and Spice Mixes

Note 1: The same recipe may be used with red or yellow bell peppers.

SIMPLIFIED CHICKEN CURRY RECIPE #1

The next several recipes are simple recipes for making chicken curry. I am following an eighty-twenty rule for these recipes under the "Simple" heading. The idea is to make 100% healthy dishes using ingredients (such as spices and herbs) that have been proven over the years to have immense health benefits and retain at least 80% yumminess of the original dish BUT with only 20% of the effort.

This recipe is a simplified Kerala (a southern state in India) style chicken curry. The authentic recipe is quite detailed. I tried to make it simple using only the ingredients below.

Ingredients

- 2 lbs. chicken breast cut into small (1 inch) pieces
- 1-2 tsp of curry powder
- 1/2 tsp turmeric
- 2 medium onion chopped
- 2-3 tsp coconut oil
- ½ tsp pepper powder
- 2 tbsp ginger garlic paste (or 1 tbsp ginger paste and 1 tbsp garlic paste)
- 1 springs of curry leaves
- 2 medium tomatoes, chopped
- 1 tsp lime juice

CURRY: Curry Powder and Spice Mixes

Method
1. Sprinkle ½ teaspoon curry powder, turmeric, lime juice, and ¼ teaspoon salt on cut chicken. Mix well and keep it aside for 30 minutes.
2. In a separate pan, heat oil and sauté onions, garlic, and ginger until onions become translucent.
3. Add remaining curry powder, pepper powder, coriander, and cumin and mix for 1-2 minutes so the spices are cooked. Make sure not to burn spices.
4. Add chicken and mix it on high heat for one minute so that any raw spices sticking to the chicken as the marinade get fried in oil and also so the chicken pieces are well coated with spices and herbs. Add tomatoes, cover and cook for 15-20 minutes on low heat. No need to add water. The moisture in the chicken and tomatoes is enough. Stir occasionally.
5. Once the chicken is cooked, add cilantro and stir. Add salt to taste. Switch off the heat and keep it covered for 1-2 minutes before serving.

Serve with rice or bread.

SIMPLIFIED CHICKEN CURRY RECIPE #2

This recipe is another simplified Kerala (a southern state in India) style chicken curry. This curry is made with coconut milk. As before, the authentic recipe is quite detailed.

Ingredients

- 2 lbs. chicken thighs and legs, bone-in

CURRY: Curry Powder and Spice Mixes

- 1-2 tsp of curry powder, depending on your tolerance to spice
- 2 tbsp coriander powder
- 2 medium onions, chopped
- 2-3 tsp coconut oil
- 1 tsp pepper powder
- ½ tsp cumin powder
- 2 tbsp ginger garlic paste (or 1 tbsp ginger paste and 1 tbsp garlic paste)
- 1 can coconut milk
- ¼ teaspoon salt
- 1 tsp lime juice
- 2 springs of curry leaves

Method

1. Sprinkle ½ tsp curry powder, turmeric, lime juice, and ¼ tsp salt on cut chicken. Mix well and keep aside for 30 minutes.
2. In a separate pan, heat oil and add curry leaves and immediately add onions, garlic, and ginger and sauté until onions become translucent. Be careful when curry leaves are added, as it may splatter hot oil.
3. Add remaining curry powder, pepper powder, coriander, and cumin and mix for 1-2 minutes so the spices are cooked. Make sure not to burn spices.
4. Add chicken and mix it on high heat for one minute so that any raw spices sticking to the chicken as marinade gets fried in oil and also the chicken pieces are well coated with spices and herbs. Add tomato, cover, and cook for 15-20 minutes on low flame. There is no need

to add water, the moisture in chicken and tomato is enough. Stir occasionally.
5. Once the chicken is cooked, add coconut milk and stir well. Add salt to taste. Add mint leaves. Switch off the heat and keep it covered for 1-2 minutes before serving.

Serve with rice or bread.

SIMPLIFIED CHICKEN CURRY RECIPE #3

This recipe is another simplified chicken curry recipe. By now, you may have noticed that you can make a number of simple or easy chicken curries by altering the ingredients in the curry slightly. You can apply your creativity to vary the amount of spices or the spice/herb combinations and even the cooking medium (coconut/vegetable/olive/butter) and get delicious and different curry results.

Ingredients

- 2 lbs. chicken thighs and legs bone-in
- 1-2 tsp of mild curry powder, depending on your tolerance on spice
- 2 tbsp coriander powder
- ½ tsp turmeric powder
- 2 medium onion chopped
- 2-3 tsp coconut oil
- ½ tsp garam masala
- ½ tsp cumin powder
- 2 tbsp ginger garlic paste (or 1 tbsp ginger paste and 1 tbsp garlic paste)
- 2 medium potatoes peeled and cut

CURRY: Curry Powder and Spice Mixes

- 2-3 medium tomatoes sliced
- Salt to taste
- ½ -1 can of chicken broth (depending on the amount gravy desired)
- ½ cup cilantro chopped

Method

1. Sprinkle ½ tsp curry powder, turmeric, and ¼ tsp salt on cut chicken. Mix well and keep it aside for 30 minutes.
2. In a separate pan, heat oil, sauté onions, garlic, curry leaves, and ginger until onions become translucent.
3. Add remaining curry powder, and also the other spices and mix for 1-2 minutes so the spices are cooked. Make sure not to burn spices.
4. Add potatoes, mix well and cook covered for 5 minutes or until potatoes are tender. Now add chicken and mix it on high heat for one minute so that any raw spices sticking to the chicken as marinade gets fried in oil and also the chicken pieces are well coated with spices and herbs. Add tomato, cover, and cook for 15-20 minutes on low flame. Add enough chicken broth for the desired thickness. Stir occasionally.
5. Once the chicken and potatoes are cooked, add cilantro and stir. Add salt to taste. Switch off the heat and keep it covered for 1-2 minutes before serving.

Serve with rice or bread.

EGG CURRY RECIPE #1 (SIMPLE VERSION)

CURRY: Curry Powder and Spice Mixes

Ingredients

- 4 fresh eggs
- 1-2 tsp curry powder (mild, medium or hot depending on your tolerance level)
- 1 tsp lemon juice
- ½ inch ginger, finely chopped
- 2 medium onions chopped
- 3 medium tomatoes sliced
- 2 tsp coconut or vegetable oil
- ½ cup cilantro, chopped
- Salt to taste
- 1 cup chicken or vegetable broth

Method

1. Make a paste by combining lemon juice and 1 tsp water with the curry powder.
2. Heat oil in a non-stick pan over medium heat.
3. Add mustard and cumin and after it crackles (5-10 seconds), add onions and ginger and sauté until onions become translucent.
4. Add the curry paste and sauté it well so the spices are cooked. Make sure it does not stick to the bottom.
5. Add tomatoes and cilantro. Mix well. Cover and cook on low flame for 15 minutes. If needed, stir occasionally so it does not stick to the pan.
6. Add chicken or vegetable broth and bring to a boil.
7. Now crack the eggs and pour directly on top of the boiling curry, spacing them separately.
8. Use a spoon and pour some of the curry sauce on top of the eggs so the eggs get soaked in gravy.

9. Cover and simmer for 10 minutes or until eggs are cooked on low heat.

Serve with rice or bread.

Egg Curry Recipe #2

Ingredients

- 4 hard-boiled eggs peeled and cut into halves
- ½ tsp cayenne pepper
- ½ tsp turmeric powder
- 1 tsp coriander powder
- ¼ black pepper powder
- 1 tsp cumin powder
- ½ inch ginger, finely chopped
- 2 medium onions chopped
- 3 medium tomatoes sliced
- 2 tsp coconut or vegetable oil
- ½ cup cilantro, chopped
- Salt to taste
- ¼ teaspoon brown sugar (optional)
- 1 cup chicken or vegetable broth

Method

1. Heat oil in a non-stick pan over medium heat.
2. Add cumin and after it crackles (5-10 seconds), add onions and ginger and sauté until onions become translucent.

3. Add the spices and sauté it well so the spices are cooked. Make sure it does not stick to the bottom.
4. Add tomatoes, cilantro, and optional sugar. Mix well. Cover and cook on low flame for 15 minutes. If needed, stir occasionally so it does not stick to the pan.
5. Lay the cut eggs on top of the sauce in the pan. Use a spoon and pour some of the curry sauce on top of the eggs so the egg pieces get soaked in gravy.
6. Cover and simmer for 2-3 minutes. Add salt to taste.

Serve with rice or bread.

LENTIL CURRY RECIPES

Legumes and lentils are some of the healthiest foods by virtue of their low fat and low sugar. They are also high in fiber and protein. Lentils are even more important as a source of protein as part of a vegan diet. Some lentil varieties, such as black beans, have anti-cancer properties. Lentils are also beneficial as part of a diet that helps with weight loss, a healthy heart, or lowering cholesterol.

Cooking lentils is pretty easy. Lentils being dried grains, it takes more time to cook than regular vegetables. The easiest way to cook lentils to soak them in water before cooking them. A one pot electric pressure cooker or manual cooker can cut cooking down into half and also cook them much better than the regular stovetop cooking.

There are literally hundreds of recipes for making lentil-based curry depending on the type of lentil and spices and herbs used, and any other vegetables added in making the curry.

CURRY: Curry Powder and Spice Mixes

Whole or split lentil may be used for making lentil curry. Typically, lentil curry is prepared with lentils as the only ingredient other than spices and herbs sautéed with onions. The following vegetables may be added while cooking lentils to make different lentil preparations:

- Tomatoes
- Potatoes
- Celery
- Carrots
- Spinach
- Cabbage
- Bell peppers
- Eggplants
- Snake gourd
- Okra
- Broccoli
- Cauliflower
- Butternut squash
- Pumpkins
- Beans
- Peas
- A mix of other legumes
- Various types of gourds

The simplest way to add these veggies to lentils is to cook them together in a pressure cooker. The vegetables will get cooked very well along with the lentils and will enhance the overall nutrition and flavor. You can add one or more of these vegetables but keep the proportion to 1 cup lentil to 2 cups or less of vegetables to keep the lentil curry more balanced.

CURRY: Curry Powder and Spice Mixes

Curry powder blend or paste of your choice or individual spices may be used in the preparation of lentil curry. The same preparation may be used for other legumes such as chickpeas, peas, kidney beans, and more.

By using different spice blends, one can create different versions of lentil curry. In its simplest form, cooked lentil is mixed with onions sautéed in coconut or vegetable oil with a teaspoon of turmeric.

Below are several recipes.

LENTIL CURRY RECIPE #1 (SIMPLE VERSION)

Ingredients

- 2 cups of red lentils (split or whole)
- 1-2 tsp curry powder (mild, medium or hot depending on your tolerance level)
- 1 tsp turmeric powder
- ¼ black pepper powder
- 2 medium onions chopped
- 2 tbsp lemon juice
- 2 tsp coconut or vegetable oil
- ½ cup cilantro, chopped
- Salt to taste
- 5-6 cups of water

Method

1. Wash lentils and put them in a one pot electric or manual pressure cooker. Add turmeric and pepper

powder. Add 5-6 cups of water. Cook in beans setting (electric pressure cooker) or until steam blows off 2-3 times in a manual pressure cooker. Switch off and let it cool down.
2. Heat oil in a pan. Add onions and sauté until onions become translucent.
3. Add curry powder and sauté for 3-4 minutes or until the curry powder gets fried with onions.
4. Add the cooked lentil. Mix it well. Bring it to a boil. Add cilantro, lemon juice, and salt to taste. Stir well.
5. Switch off and lentil curry is ready.

Lentil Curry Recipe #2

Ingredients

- 2 cups of red lentils (split or whole)
- 1-2 tsp curry powder (mild, medium or hot depending on your tolerance level)
- 1 tsp cumin
- 1 tsp turmeric powder
- ¼ black pepper powder
- 1 jalapeño split lengthwise
- 2 medium onions, chopped
- 3 medium tomatoes, sliced
- 2 cups of celery, chopped
- 2 tsp coconut or vegetable oil
- ½ cup cilantro, chopped
- Salt to taste
- 5-6 cups of water

CURRY: Curry Powder and Spice Mixes

Method

1. Wash lentils and put them in a one pot electric or manual pressure cooker. Add turmeric and pepper powder. Add jalapeños, tomatoes and celery. Add 5-6 cups of water. Cook in beans setting (electric pressure cooker) or until steam blows off 2-3 times in a manual pressure cooker. Switch off and let it cool down.
2. Heat oil in a pan. Crackle cumin. Add onions and sauté until onions become translucent.
3. Add curry powder and sauté for 3-4 minutes or until the curry powder gets fried with onions.
4. Add the cooked lentil. Mix it well. Bring it to a boil. Add cilantro. Switch off and serve with rice or bread.

LENTIL AND SPINACH CURRY

Ingredients

- 1 cups of red lentils (split or whole)
- 2 bunches of spinach, washed and chopped
- 1-2 tsp curry powder (mild, medium or hot depending on your tolerance level)
- 1 tsp cumin
- 1 tsp turmeric powder
- ¼ black pepper powder
- 1 jalapeño split lengthwise
- 2 medium onions, chopped
- 3 medium tomatoes, sliced
- 2 tsp coconut or vegetable oil
- ½ cup cilantro, chopped
- Salt to taste
- 5-6 cups of water

Method

1. Wash lentils and put it in one pot electric or manual pressure cooker. Add turmeric and pepper powder. Add jalapeños, tomatoes, and spinach. Add 5-6 cups of water. Cook in beans setting (electric pressure cooker) or until steam blows off 2-3 times in a manual pressure cooker. Switch and let it cool down.
2. Heat oil in a pan. Crackle cumin. Add onions and sauté until onions become translucent.
3. Add curry powder and sauté for 3-4 minutes or until the curry powder gets fried with onions.
4. Add the cooked lentil and spinach. Mix it well. Bring it to a boil and add cilantro.
5. Switch off and lentil curry is ready.

QUICK AND EASY CHICKPEAS CURRY

Ingredients

- 1 cup chickpeas soaked in water overnight
- 1 cup curry paste
- 1 tsp cumin
- 2 medium onions, chopped
- 2 tsp coconut or vegetable oil
- ½ cup cilantro, chopped
- Salt to taste
- 3 cups of water

Method

1. Cook the chickpeas in a pressure cooker with 3-4 cups of water and set aside.
2. Heat oil in a pan. Crackle cumin. Add onions and sauté until onions become translucent.
3. Add curry paste. Mix it well. Add cilantro.
4. Now add the chickpeas and bring to a boil.
5. Turn off the heat and lentil curry is done.

QUICK AND EASY CANNED GARBANZO BEANS CURRY

Ingredients

- 2 cans of garbanzo beans
- 1 cup curry paste
- ½ cup cilantro, chopped
- Salt to taste

Method

1. In a pan mix the garbanzo beans with curry paste.
2. Bring it to a boil. Add ½ cup water if needed.
3. Add cilantro. Cover and simmer for 5 minutes.
4. Turn off the heat and lentil curry is done.

EASY THAI RED CURRY CHICKEN

Ingredients

- 6-8 boneless chicken thighs cut into pieces

CURRY: Curry Powder and Spice Mixes

- 1 tbsp coconut oil
- 1 tbsp ginger-garlic paste
- ¼ cup or 4 tbsp red curry paste
- 2 cans of coconut milk
- ¼ cup Thai basil chopped
- ½ inch piece of ginger
- 2 Lime leaves

Method

1. Heat oil in a large pan over medium heat, sauté ginger-garlic paste for about a minute. Add Thai red curry paste and mix for another minute.
2. Add coconut milk and bring it a boil.
3. Add chicken and lime leaves. Bring to a boil and simmer covered for 10-15 minutes or until chicken is cooked.
4. Add Thai basil. Mix. Switch off the heat. Keep it covered for a couple of minutes before serving.

EASY THAI RED CURRY VEGETABLES

Ingredients

- 4-5 baby corns
- 1 cup mushrooms
- 1 cup eggplant cut into inch long pieces
- 1 cup broccoli florets
- ½ cup tomato, chopped
- 1 tbsp coconut oil
- 1 tbsp ginger-garlic paste

CURRY: Curry Powder and Spice Mixes

- ¼ cup or 4 tbsp red curry paste
- 2 cans of coconut milk
- ¼ cup Thai basil, chopped
- ½ inch piece of ginger
- 2 Lime leaves
- ¼ tsp black pepper powder
- Salt to taste

Method

1. Heat oil in a large pan over medium heat, sauté ginger-garlic paste for about a minute. Add Thai red curry paste and mix for another minute. Add tomatoes and mix. Add pepper powder.
2. Add coconut milk and bring to a boil.
3. Add all the vegetables and lime leaves. Bring to a boil and simmer covered for 10-15 minutes or until vegetables are cooked.
4. Add Thai basil and mix. Switch off the heat.
5. Keep it covered for a couple of minutes before serving.

Notes:

1. 1 cup chicken breast cut into pieces may be added to make this a chicken and vegetable Thai curry.
2. You can make the Thai red curry paste as described in this book or buy off the shelf from Asian stores or online.
3. You can try adding 1 tsp soy sauce and/or 1 tsp vinegar. Should you like the taste you can make it as part of the recipe.

| CURRY: Curry Powder and Spice Mixes

4. Try adding 1 tsp brown sugar and see if you like it. If you do, you can add it as part of the recipe.

Mutton Curry Recipe #1

Basic Ingredients

- 2 mutton cut into pieces
- 1-2-inch ginger chopped
- 2 medium onions chopped
- 2 medium tomatoes chopped
- 2 medium potatoes peeled and cubed
- 1-2 tbsp mild curry powder
- 6-12 cloves of garlic
- 2-3 tbsp coconut or vegetable oil
- 1 bay leaf or 1 curry leaf stalk
- 1-2 tbsp garam masala powder
- 2 tbsp ginger garlic paste (to make marinade)
- 1 tbsp coriander powder (to make marinade)
- 1 tbsp cumin powder (to make marinade)
- ½ cup non-fat yogurt (to make marinade)
- ½ cup cilantro (to garnish)
- Salt to taste

Method

1. Mix yogurt, salt, turmeric, ginger-garlic paste, cumin powder, and coriander powder together in a bowl to make the marinade. Marinate the mutton with this paste for about two hours or overnight.

2. Add ¾ of the chopped onions, ginger and garlic and tomatoes to a food processor or blender and make a puree and keep it aside.
3. In a pressure cooker or one pot (medium heat for the pressure cooker or sauté setting for the electric one pot), add oil and sauté onions for a couple of minutes or until they become translucent. Add all spices and stir well for about 1 minute to cook the spices in oil.
4. Add the marinated mutton pieces, potatoes, bay leaf, and curry leaves. Mix well for a couple of minutes.
5. Add the pureed ingredients and mix well. Close the lid of the cooker and pressure cook the mutton for 2-3 whistles or on meat setting in an electric cooker.
6. When done, let the steam release on its own, garnish with chopped coriander leaves.

Recipe Notes:

1. Usually, there is enough water content to get the mutton cooked in a one pot electric cooker. If you are using the traditional pressure cooker, you may want to add ½ - 1 cup water before closing the lid and cooking.

Mutton Curry Recipe #2

Basic Ingredients

CURRY: Curry Powder and Spice Mixes

- 2 lbs. mutton cut into pieces
- 1-2-inch ginger
- 3 medium tomatoes, chopped
- 1-2 tbsp mild curry powder
- 6-12 cloves of garlic
- 2-3 tbsp coconut or vegetable oil
- 1 bay leaf or 1 curry leaf stalk
- 1-2 tbsp garam masala powder
- 4 cloves
- 4 cardamom
- 1-inch cinnamon
- 2 tbsp ginger garlic paste (to make marinade)
- 1 tbsp coriander powder (to make marinade)
- 1 tbsp cumin powder (to make marinade)
- ½ cup non-fat yogurt (to make marinade)
- ½ cup cilantro (to garnish)
- Salt to taste

Method

1. Put all the mutton pieces into a bowl, add the marinade ingredients, mix well, rubbing the spices into the meat. Marinate for 1-2 hours or overnight.
2. Heat oil in a pan. Add the chopped onions and cook on low flame for 10 minutes.
3. When the onions turn translucent, add whole spices and spice powders and mix well.
4. Now add the marinated mutton and the ginger garlic paste and cook on high heat for 5-7 minutes, stirring continuously.
5. Cover and cook on low the flame and allow it to simmer for 20-25 minutes or until mutton is cooked.
6. Garnish with coriander leaves and serve hot with steamed rice or bread.

THAI COCONUT CURRY NOODLE SOUP (CHICKEN)

Ingredients

- ½ lb. boneless chicken thighs or breast cut into small pieces
- 1 tbsp coconut oil
- 4 cloves of garlic chopped
- 1-inch ginger grated
- ¼ cup or 4 tbsp red curry paste
- 1 can (2 cups) of coconut milk
- 1-1/2 can (3 cups) of chicken broth
- ¼ cup Thai basil chopped
- 200 grams (7 oz) vermicelli rice noodles
- 2 tbsp fish sauce
- 1 medium tomato sliced
- ¼ cup cilantro
- 2 tsp lime juice (optional)
- Salt to taste
- Green onions chopped to garnish

Method

1. Heat oil in a large pan over medium heat, sauté ginger and garlic paste for about a minute. Add Thai red curry paste and fry for about 3-4 minutes.
2. Add chicken pieces and cook for another 5 minutes stirring well until chicken is coated with the curry paste and turns opaque.
3. Add chicken broth, coconut milk, and fish sauce. Bring it to a boil. Taste and add salt if needed.
4. Add Thai basil. Mix. Now add the noodles. Bring it to a boil. Switch off and keep it covered for a couple of

minutes. Add cilantro and optional lime juice and serve.

Thai Coconut Curry Noodle Soup (vegan)

Ingredients

- 1 tbsp coconut oil
- 3 cloves of garlic chopped
- 1-inch ginger grated
- 2 tbsp red curry paste
- 1 can (2 cups) of coconut milk
- 1-1/2 can (3 cups) of vegetable broth
- ¼ cup Thai basil, chopped
- 200 grams (7 oz) vermicelli rice noodles
- 1 medium tomato, sliced
- 1 jalapeno sliced lengthwise into 4 pieces (optional)
- ¼ cup cilantro
- 2 tsp lime juice (optional)
- Salt to taste
- Green onions, chopped (to garnish)

Method

1. Heat oil in a large pan over medium heat, sauté ginger and garlic paste for about a minute. Add Thai red curry paste, and jalapenos and fry for about 3-4 minutes.
2. Add the tomato and cook for another 5 minutes stirring well.
3. Add vegetable broth and coconut milk. Bring it to a boil. Taste and add salt if needed.
4. Add Thai basil. Mix. Add the noodles and bring it to a boil.

CURRY: Curry Powder and Spice Mixes

5. Switch off and keep it covered for a couple of minutes. Add cilantro, chopped green onions and optional lime juice and serve.

QUICK AND EASY DORO WAT (ETHIOPIAN CHICKEN CURRY)

Ingredients

- 3 lbs. chicken breasts cut into 1 inch pieces
- 6-8 chicken drumsticks
- 3 cups yellow onions, finely minced
- 3 tablespoons butter
- 1 tablespoon finely minced garlic
- 1 tablespoon finely minced ginger
- 1/4 cup or 4 tablespoons berbere mix
- 1 tsp salt or to taste
- 1/4 cup chicken broth
- 6 hard-boiled eggs cut into half

Method 1 (using a one pot or electric pressure cooker)

1. Put the pressure cooker on sauté (electric) or on medium heat. Melt butter, add the berbere and stir well.
2. Add the onions, garlic and ginger, and sauté and cook the mixture for 5-10 minutes.
3. Add chicken legs and stir well to coat the chicken with the berbere, onion, garlic, and ginger mix.

| CURRY: Curry Powder and Spice Mixes

4. Add the chicken broth, seal cooker, and cook on poultry or until pressure builds and steam escapes (for manual cooker)
5. Add hard-boiled egg halves and stir gently before serving.

Recipe Notes:

1. In most cases chicken releases juice during pressure cooking, which means there may be no need for adding chicken broth.
2. In case the doro wat is too "watery", open the pressure cooker lid and let it simmer for some time, so the sauce thickens.
3. Authentic doro wat is slow-cooked over several hours and instead of butter, Niter Kibbeh is used.

Method 2 (using a saucepan)

1. Melt Niter Kibbeh or butter in a saucepan.
2. Add the onions, garlic, and ginger, and sauté until onions are golden brown.
3. Add berbere mix and stir well. Cook for 5-10 minutes
4. Add chicken legs and stir well to coat the chicken with the berbere and onion, garlic, and ginger mix.
5. Add the chicken broth, cook covered for 25-35 minutes stirring occasionally so the mix does not stick to the bottom
6. Add hard-boiled egg halves and stir gently before serving.

Eggplant Curry (Vegan)

Ingredients

- 1 large eggplant coconut oil
- 3 cloves of garlic, chopped
- 1 cup finely chopped onions
- 1 cup finely chopped tomatoes
- ¼ tsp chili powder (use mild, medium or hot depending on your heat tolerance level)
- ½ tsp garam masala
- ¼ cup cilantro
- 2 tsp lime juice (optional)
- Salt to taste

Method

1. Flame or oven roast the eggplant. In the oven, use the broil setting to get the eggplant cooked and the skin charred. Make sure to turn the eggplant over so the cooking is even all around. If you are using an open flame, use the same guideline to cook it evenly and get the skin charred so it can be peeled off easily.
2. Let the eggplant cool down. Peel the skin away and mash the remaining eggplant into a fine mixture.
3. Heat oil in a non-stick pan and sauté onions until golden brown. Add chili powder and garam masala and mix well. Add tomatoes and cook well until oil separates.

4. Add mashed eggplant and mix well. Lower the heat and cook covered for about 5 minutes. Add cilantro, and lime juice, mix well, and serve hot.

MIXED VEGETABLE CURRY (VEGAN)

Ingredients

- 3 cups of mixed vegetables of your choice (a combination of three or more of peas, carrots, beans, cauliflower, potatoes, bell pepper, or beetroots)
- 1 cup finely chopped onions
- 1 cup finely chopped tomatoes
- ½ tsp cumin seeds
- 1 tsp ginger garlic paste
- ½ tsp garam masala
- ½ - 1 tsp curry powder
- ¼ tsp turmeric powder
- ¼ - ½ tsp chili powder
- 1 sliced green chili seeds out
- ¼ cup cilantro
- Salt to taste
- Vegetable broth or water as required

Method

1. Heat oil in a non-stick pan and sauté cumin seeds until they crackle. Add onions and fry until golden brown.

CURRY: Curry Powder and Spice Mixes

2. Add ginger-garlic paste, chili powder, curry powder, and turmeric and mix well.
3. Add tomatoes and cook well until oil separates.
4. Add mixed vegetables and mix well. Sauté the vegetables for 2-3 minutes so the vegetable pieces are well coated with the spice mix.
5. Add about ½ cup vegetable broth or water so there is just enough liquid for the vegetables to cook.
6. Cover and cook on low-medium heat for 10-15 minutes or until vegetables are cooked well.
7. Add cilantro and salt. Mix well and serve hot with Indian bread or rice.

VEGETABLE KORMA

Vegetable korma is a creamy Indian mixed vegetable curry primarily made in the northern part of India. There are several varieties of vegetable korma. Some are very rich (such as navaratan korma) and some are very light. The various recipes use various bases for the creamy part of the korma, starting from heavy cream to yogurt, to cashew puree or coconut milk. Most recipes use powdered spices and the spice mix differs used differs based on taste and spice tolerance levels.

Ingredients

To make the puree
- 1 cup finely chopped onions
- ¼ cup cashews
- 1 cinnamon stick inch long
- 2-3 cardamom pods

CURRY: Curry Powder and Spice Mixes

- 3-4 garlic cloves
- 1-inch ginger peeled and grated
- 1 jalapeno peppers, seeded and sliced

To make korma

- 3 cups of mixed vegetables of your choice (a combination of three or more of peas, carrots, beans, cauliflower, potatoes, bell pepper, or beetroots)
- 1 cup finely chopped tomatoes
- ½ tsp garam masala
- ½ - 1 tsp curry powder
- ½ tsp turmeric powder
- ¼ - ½ tsp chili powder
- ½ tsp coriander powder
- ½ tsp black pepper powder
- ¼ cup cilantro
- Salt to taste
- ½ cup coconut milk (unsweetened)
- ½ cup plain yogurt
- 1 tbsp coconut oil
- 2-3 teaspoons brown sugar (optional)

Method

1. Blend all the items for the puree in a food processor or blender and set it aside. Add a bit of water if needed so it blends well.
2. Heat oil in a non-stick pan and sauté the pureed ingredients in oil. Use caution not to splatter the puree in oil.

3. Add all the spice powders and mix well. Let it cook for 2-3 minutes on low heat. Stir well so the spices do not stick to the bottom.
4. Add tomatoes and mixed vegetables and mix well. Sauté the vegetables for 2-3 minutes so the vegetable pieces are well coated with the spice mix.
5. Add coconut milk and yogurt. Cover and allow it to simmer on low-medium heat for 10-15 minutes or until vegetables are cooked well. Stir occasionally.
6. Add cilantro, salt, and optional brown sugar. Mix well and serve hot with Indian bread or basmati rice.

Yogurt Curry

This is a popular curry in Indian cooking and has several different variations. The simplest version of the recipe is below.

Basic Ingredients

- 1 teaspoon turmeric powder
- ½ inch – 1-inch fresh ginger, grated or thinly sliced
- 2-3 cloves of garlic, chopped
- 1 pinch of black pepper powder
- 2 cups of yogurt whisked
- 1 medium onion, finely chopped
- 2 tsp coconut (or vegetable) oil
- Salt to taste

Optional Ingredients

- ¼ cup cilantro or curry leaves, chopped
- 1 tsp mustard seeds
- 1 tsp cumin seeds
- 2 crushed red chilies

Method:

1. Heat oil in a medium non-stick pan, add optional mustard seeds, cumin, and red chilies and let it crackle
2. Add onions, ginger, garlic, and optional curry leaves or cilantro.
3. Stir until golden and add turmeric and black pepper, stir for one minute and then add the yogurt and mix well. Switch off the heat and enjoy it with rice.

SALMON WITH GREEN MANGO

Basic Ingredients

- 2lb skinless salmon, cleaned and cut into 2-inch pieces
- 1-4 tsp chili powder, (depending on your tolerance level)
- 1 tsp turmeric powder
- 1 tsp coriander powder
- ¼ tsp fenugreek powder or ½ tsp fenugreek seeds
- ¼ tsp black pepper powder
- ½ tsp mustard seeds
- 1 medium onion sliced
- 2 tsp ginger grated
- 4-5 cloves garlic crushed

CURRY: Curry Powder and Spice Mixes

- 2 cups green mango cashed and cut into 1-inch pieces (with skin or skin removed depending on your preference)
- 1 to 1 ½ cups water (or as required)
- Salt to taste

Optional Ingredients

- 2 springs of curry leaves
- 2-4 sliced green chilies or jalapeños, seeds removed

Method

1. Combine all the spice powders–chili, turmeric, coriander, fenugreek, and pepper powder together in a bowl. Add 2 tsp or just enough water to make a thick paste and set aside.
2. Heat oil in a pan and splutter mustard seeds and fenugreek (if seeds are used instead of powder).
3. Add ginger, garlic, onion, and optional green chilies and curry leaves. Sauté until onion becomes translucent.
4. Add the masala paste and mix well on low flame (wet the masala to make sure it gets fried but not burnt).
5. After a few minutes (once masala gets fried), add about 2 cups of water, mix, and then add the cut mango pieces.
6. Cover and bring it to a boil on medium heat. Now add individual fish pieces into the pan.
7. Mix gently, making sure the fish pieces are not broken up and that all the pieces are coated with the gravy.

8. Cover the pan and cook it for about 20 minutes or until fish is done and the gravy is thick. Switch off the flame and keep it covered for 30 minutes for the fish to soak in the spices and mango flavor.

Serve with rice or bread.

Notes:

1. Paprika may be used instead of chili powder if you desire to make it less spicy.
2. Any other fish may be used instead of salmon.
3. Instead of mango, tamarind or *Garcinia cambogia* (the scientific name for the black tamarind available in Asian stores) may be used.
4. Green chilies or jalapeños add more heat to the fish curry. Use them depending on your taste.

QUICK AND EASY SHRIMP & GREEN BEANS MASALA

Basic Ingredients

- 1 lbs. shrimp cleaned
- 1-inch fresh ginger grated or thinly sliced
- 2-3 cloves of garlic crushed
- 1 tsp curry powder
- ½ tsp chili powder
- 1 tsp paprika
- 1 large onion, finely chopped
- 2 tsp coconut (or vegetable) oil
- 2 cup green beans cut into ½ inch pieces
- Salt to taste
- 1 tbsp lime juice

CURRY: Curry Powder and Spice Mixes

Optional Ingredients

- ¼ cup cilantro or curry leaves, chopped
- 1 tsp mustard seeds
- 1-2 green chilies/jalapenos
- 1 tsp cumin seeds
- 1 spring of curry leaves
- 2 tomatoes, sliced

Method:

1. Heat oil in a medium non-stick pan, add optional mustard seeds and cumin and let it crackle. Add optional curry leaves and fry for 2-3 seconds to release the aroma.
2. Add onions, ginger, garlic, and optional chilies. Sauté until golden.
3. Add all the spice powders. Mix for a couple of minutes until they're fried. Add optional tomatoes; mix.
4. Add shrimp and beans. Stir so the shrimp and beans are mixed well with the spices and onions.
5. Cover and cook in low-medium heat for 15-20 minutes or until beans and shrimp are cooked well. Mix well so as not to stick to the bottom. Switch off the heat and add optional cilantro and lime juice.

Notes

CURRY: Curry Powder and Spice Mixes

1. Usually there will be enough water from the shrimp and optional tomatoes for the dish to cook. If the masala is too dry add ¼ cup water while cooking.
2. You can make shrimp masala without beans. Follow the same recipe. You may want to adjust down the spices if you chose not to add beans.
3. To reduce the heat, you can change the proportion of chili powder and paprika (less chili powder and more paprika)

THAI GREEN CURRY CHICKEN

Basic Ingredients

- 1.5 lbs. boneless chicken breast or thighs cut into ½ inch pieces
- 1/2 cup Thai green curry paste
- 1 cup green beans (whole or cut into half)
- 1 cup broccoli
- 1 cup coconut milk
- ½ inch ginger, sliced into long pieces
- ½ cup cilantro
- 2 tsp coconut (or vegetable) oil
- 1 sliced green chili
- Salt to taste
- 1 tsp lime juice

Method
1. Heat oil in a non-stick pan, add the green curry paste, green chilies, and ginger, and fry it for 1-2 minutes stirring well.
2. Add chicken, beans, and broccoli. Mix well.

3. Add coconut milk; cover and cook for 15-20 minutes or until the vegetables and chicken are cooked. Add ½-1 cup chicken broth if required.
4. Garnish with cilantro and serve with Jasmine rice.

Notes:

1. You can use the green curry paste made using the recipes given in this book or buy off the shelf from Asian or online stores.
2. You can also add some lemongrass to enhance the flavor.

THAI PORK AND PEANUT CURRY

Basic Ingredients

- 1 lbs. pork cut into ½ inch pieces
- 1/2 cup Thai red curry paste
- ½ cup peanut butter
- 2 cup coconut milk
- ½ cup cilantro
- 2 tsp coconut (or vegetable) oil
- Salt to taste
- 1 tbsp. lime juice
- 1 tbsp soy sauce
- ½ cup chopped green onions
- 1 tbsp brown sugar (optional)

Method

CURRY: Curry Powder and Spice Mixes

1. Heat oil in a large non-stick pan over medium heat. Sauté chopped green onions for a couple of minutes. Add pork and cook for 5-7 minutes stirring continuously.

2. Add Thai red curry paste, peanut butter and optional brown sugar, soy sauce, coconut milk, and water. Mix well. Cover and cook for about 10-15 minutes or until pork is cooked.

3. Add the lime juice and mix well. Garnish with cilantro and serve with rice.

STREET FOOD STYLE SPICY CHICKEN CURRY

Ingredients

- 1.5 lbs. bone-in chicken cut into small pieces
- ¼ teaspoon cinnamon
- 2 cloves
- One large finely chopped onion
- ½ teaspoon ginger paste
- ½ teaspoon garlic paste
- ½ teaspoon coriander powder
- 1 teaspoon cumin powder
- 5-6 soaked cashews or almonds
- 1 spring curry leaves (optional)
- 4 red whole red chilies (optional)
- 1 tablespoon coconut or olive oil
- 2 medium tomato chopped
- 1 ½ teaspoon powdered black pepper

CURRY: Curry Powder and Spice Mixes

To marinate:

- ½ cup yogurt
- ½ teaspoon turmeric powder
- ½ teaspoon red chili powder
- ½ teaspoon salt

To garnish (optional)

- 3-4 lemon slices/wedges
- ¼ cup onion slices
- ½ teaspoon parsley, chopped
- 1 teaspoon coriander leaves, chopped

Method

1. Make a marinade by mixing yogurt, turmeric powder, and chili powder. In a large enough bowl, apply marinade on the chicken pieces. Mix it well and keep it aside at least 2 for hours, preferably overnight.

2. Heat oil in a pan on medium heat. Add chopped onions and sauté for a few minutes or until onions become translucent. Add the ginger-garlic paste, coriander powder, black pepper powder, and cumin powder. Mix well for a minute and then add chopped tomatoes and cashews. Let it cook it for 2-3 minutes or until the oil starts to separate. Switch off the heat and let it cool down.

3. Grind the sautéed mix from step 2 and set aside.

4. Heat the remaining oil in a saucepan and add optional whole chilies and curry leaves. Fry them for

CURRY: Curry Powder and Spice Mixes

a few seconds and then add marinated chicken pieces. Mix well. Cover and cook for 5-6 minutes.

5. Add the ground mixture. Mix well and cook covered for another 5-10 minutes on low heat or until the chicken pieces are tender.

6. Add salt to taste. Garnish with cilantro, parsley, lemon wedges, and onion slices.

Butter Chicken

Ingredients

- 2lbs. chicken breast cut into 1-inch pieces
- One large finely chopped onion
- ½ teaspoon ginger paste
- ½ teaspoon garlic paste
- ½ teaspoon coriander powder
- ½ teaspoon garam masala powder
- ¼ tsp cayenne pepper
- 1 teaspoon cumin powder
- ¼ cup cashews, soaked in water
- 1 tablespoon coconut or olive oil
- 4 medium tomatoes, chopped

To marinate:
- ½ cup yogurt
- ½ teaspoon turmeric powder
- ½ teaspoon red chili powder
- ½ teaspoon salt

CURRY: Curry Powder and Spice Mixes

- ½ tsp garam masala powder

Method

1. Make a marinade by mixing yogurt, turmeric powder, and chili powder. In a large bowl, mix the marinade with the chicken pieces. Mix it well and keep it the fridge at least 2 for hours, preferably overnight.

2. The next step is to bake or fry the marinated chicken. To bake, set the oven to 400 degrees Fahrenheit. Spread the chicken evenly on a baking tray and bake it for about 8-10 minutes, or just enough to make the chicken tender. Alternatively, add a tablespoon oil in a non-stick pan and fry the chicken pieces for about 5 minutes to make it dry and crispy.

3. Heat oil in a pan on medium heat. Add chopped onions and sauté for a few minutes or until onions become translucent. Add the ginger-garlic paste, coriander powder, black pepper powder, and cumin powder. Mix well and then add chopped tomatoes and cashews. Let it cook it for 2-3 minutes or until the oil starts to separate. Switch off the heat and let it cool down.

4. Grind the sautéed mix from step 3 and set aside.

5. Melt the butter in the saucepan and pour the blended puree back into the pan. Bring it to a boil and cook for 5 minutes or until the gravy thickens.

6. Add baked/fried chicken. Cook covered for another 5-10 minutes or until chicken is cooked and tender.

7. Add salt to taste. Garnish with cilantro and serve.

Notes:

1. If you like more creamy and rich butter chicken, add 1/3 cup of whipping cream after step 6 and mix well.
2. Optionally you can add some dried fenugreek leaves (methi) in step 5. This gives a distinct flavor.
3. Tandoori masala may be used instead of garam masala for marinating.

Chicken Tikka Masala

Ingredients

- 2lbs. chicken breast cut into 1-inch pieces

To marinate:
- 1 cup yogurt
- ½ - 1 teaspoon turmeric powder
- ½ - 1 teaspoon chili powder
- ½ teaspoon salt
- ½ teaspoon ginger paste
- 1 teaspoon garlic paste
- ½ - 1 teaspoon garam masala

For the sauce
- One large finely chopped onion
- ½ - 1 teaspoon ginger finely grated
- ½ - 1 teaspoon garlic finely chopped
- 1 teaspoon coriander powder
- ½ - 1 teaspoon garam masala powder

- ½ - 1 teaspoon cayenne pepper or Kashmiri chili powder
- ½ -2 teaspoon chili powder (optional, if you like more spicy)
- 1 teaspoon cumin powder
- 1 – 2 teaspoon turmeric powder
- 3 tablespoon coconut or olive oil
- 3 cups of tomato sauce
- 1 cup heavy cream
- 1 cup water
- 1 teaspoon brown sugar (optional)
- ¼ cup cilantro chopped

Method

1. Combine chicken with all of the ingredients for the chicken marinade; Mix well and let the chicken marinate for 30 minutes or overnight if you prefer.
2. Fry or bake the marinated chicken.
    - If you are frying, heat oil in a large pan. Add chicken pieces in batches. Fry until browned on all sides and set aside. 2-3 minutes in oil should fry them sufficiently.
    - If you are baking, pre-heat over to 450 degrees (F), bake them on a skewer in a baking pan. Bake for about 15-20 minutes or chicken becomes slightly dark brown outside.
3. Fry the onions in oil. If you had fried chicken in the previous step, the same pan and oil may be used to fry onions. If you baked, add oil and fry onions in a large pan.

CURRY: Curry Powder and Spice Mixes

4. Add garlic and ginger and sauté for 1 minute, then add garam masala, cumin, turmeric, and coriander. Fry for about 10-20 seconds until fragrant. Make sure the spices do not burn.
5. Pour in the tomato puree, chili powders, and salt. Add the fried or baked chicken along with any juices from frying/baking. Simmer for about 10-15 minutes on low heat, stir occasionally until the sauce become thick with a deep brown-red color.
6. Stir the cream and optional sugar. Cook for an additional 5 minutes or until chicken is cooked well. Add water if the sauce becomes too thick.
7. Garnish with cilantro and serve with basmati rice.

Notes:

1. Depending on your tolerance level, you can adjust the amount of spices used in this recipe.
2. The recipe is healthier than the restaurant bought tikka masala as restaurants usually use red food color to color the chicken
3. Tandoori masala may be used instead of garam masala for marinating.
4. Chili powder may be completely replaced with cayenne powder or Kashmiri chili powder. Both are milder and imparts better color to the sauce than regular chili powder.

SIMPLE CREAMED SPINACH (PALAK) CURRY

Basic Ingredients

- 1 bunch spinach, washed and dried
- 1 medium tomato, chopped

CURRY: Curry Powder and Spice Mixes

- ½ tsp cumin seeds
- ½ tsp fenugreek seeds (optional)
- ½ -1 tsp curry powder or garam masala
- 1 green chili optional
- 2 onions, finely chopped
- ½ teaspoon chopped garlic or garlic paste
- ½ teaspoon ginger, chopped, or ginger paste
- ½ teaspoon turmeric powder
- 2 tablespoon coconut oil, or olive oil

Method

1. Blend the spinach, ginger, garlic, onion, and optional green chili in a blender and keep aside.

2. Heat oil in a pan, fry the cumin seeds and optional fenugreek seeds, add curry powder or garam masala and turmeric, and stir well for a few seconds.

3. Add the spinach puree and optional chopped tomatoes. Cover and cook for 15-20 minutes, stirring occasionally so the spinach does not stick to the bottom.

4. Add salt to taste and enjoy.

REFERENCES

Curry powder history:

http://www.world-foodhistory.com/2006/12/history-of-curry-powder.html

About Garam Masala
https://en.wikipedia.org/wiki/Garam_masala

About Curry

https://en.wikipedia.org/wiki/Curry

Other references:

https://www.ncbi.nlm.nih.gov/pubmed/17569207

https://www.cancerresearchuk.org/about-cancer/cancer-in-general/treatment/complementary-alternative-therapies/individual-therapies/turmeric

https://www.alzheimers.org.uk/about-dementia/risk-factors-and-prevention/turmeric-and-dementia

https://www.sciencedirect.com/science/article/pii/S0944711308001153?via%25253Dihub

https://www.ncbi.nlm.nih.gov/pubmed/21862758

DISCLAIMER

This book details the author's personal experiences in using Indian spices, the information contained in the public domain as well as the author's opinion. The author is not licensed as a doctor, nutritionist or chef. The author is providing this book and its contents on an "as is" basis and makes no representations or warranties of any kind with respect to this book or its contents. The author disclaims all such representations and warranties, including for example warranties of merchantability and educational or medical advice for a particular purpose. In addition, the author does not represent or warrant that the information accessible via this book is accurate, complete or current. The statements made about products and services have not been evaluated by the US FDA or any equivalent organization in other countries.

The author will not be liable for damages arising out of or in connection with the use of this book or the information contained within. This is a comprehensive limitation of liability that applies to all damages of any kind, including (without limitation) compensatory; direct, indirect or consequential damages; loss of data, income or profit; loss of or damage to property and claims of third parties. It is understood that this book is not intended as a substitute for consultation with a licensed medical or a culinary professional. Before starting any lifestyle changes, it is recommended that you consult a licensed professional to ensure that you are doing what's best for your situation. The use of this book implies your acceptance of this disclaimer.

Thank You

If you enjoyed this book or found it useful, I would greatly appreciate if you could post a short review on Amazon. I read all the reviews and your feedback will help me to make this book even better. For your convenience, please click the following link to take you directly to Amazon where you can post the review.

https://www.amazon.com/dp/B07FRV1B6N

PREVIEW OF OTHER BOOKS IN THIS SERIES

ESSENTIAL SPICES AND HERBS: TURMERIC

Turmeric is truly a wonder spice. It has anti-inflammatory, anti-oxidant, anti-cancer, and anti-bacterial properties. Find out the amazing benefits of turmeric. Includes many recipes for incorporating turmeric in your daily life.

Turmeric is a spice known to man for thousands of years and has been used for cooking, food preservation, and as a natural remedy for common ailments. This book explains:

- Many health benefits of turmeric including fighting cancer, inflammation, and pain.
- Turmeric as beauty treatments - turmeric masks
- Recipes for teas, smoothies and dishes
- References and links to a number of research studies on the effectiveness of turmeric

Essential Spices and Herbs: Turmeric is a quick read and offers a lot of concise information. A great tool to have in your alternative therapies and healthy lifestyle toolbox!

PREVENTING CANCER

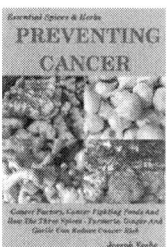

World Health Organization (WHO) estimates more than half of all cancer incidents are preventable.

Cancer is one of the most fearsome diseases to strike mankind. There has been much research into both conventional and alternative therapies for different kinds of cancers. Different cancers require different treatment options and offer a different prognosis. While there has been significant progress in recent times in cancer research towards a cure, there are none available currently. However, more than half of all cancers are likely preventable through modifications in lifestyle and diet.

Preventing Cancer offers a quick insight into cancer-causing factors, foods that fight cancer, and how the three spices, turmeric, ginger and garlic, can not only spice up your food but potentially make all your food into cancer fighting meals. While there are many other herbs and spices that help fight cancer, these three spices work together and complementarily. In addition, the medicinal value of these spices has been proven over thousands of years of use. The book includes:

- Cancer-causing factors and how to avoid them
- Top 12 cancer-fighting foods, the cancers they fight and how to incorporate them into your diet
- Cancer-fighting properties of turmeric, ginger and garlic

| CURRY: Curry Powder and Spice Mixes

- Over 30 recipes including teas, smoothies and other dishes that incorporate these spices
- References and links to many research studies on the effectiveness of these spices.

PREVENTING ALZHEIMER'S

Approximately 50 million people suffer from Alzheimer's worldwide. In the U.S. alone, 5.5 million people have Alzheimer's – about 10 percent of the worldwide Alzheimer's population.

Alzheimer's disease is a progressive brain disorder that damages and eventually destroys brain cells, leading to memory loss, changes in thinking, and other brain functions. While the rate of progressive decline in brain function is slow at the onset, it gets worse with time and age. Brain function decline accelerates, and brain cells eventually die over time. While there has been significant research done to find a cure, currently there is no cure available.

Alzheimer's incidence rate in the U.S. and other western countries is significantly higher than that of the countries in the developing world. Factors such as lifestyle, diet, physical and mental activity, and social engagement play a part in the development and progression of Alzheimer's

In most cases, if you are above the age of 50, plaques and tangles associated with Alzheimer's may have already started forming in your brain. At the age of 65, you have a 10% chance of Alzheimer's and at age 80, the chances are about 50%.

With lifestyle changes, proper diet and exercise (of the mind and body), Alzheimer's is preventable.

In recent times, Alzheimer's is beginning to reach epidemic proportions. The cost of Alzheimer's to the US economy is expected to cross a trillion dollars in 10 years. It is a serious health care issue in many of the western countries as the population age and the life expectancy increase.

At this time, our understanding of what causes Alzheimer's and the ways to treat it is at its infancy. However, we know the factors that affect Alzheimer's and we can use that knowledge to prevent, delay the onset or at least slow down the rate of progression of the disease.

While this book does not present all the answers, it is an attempt to examines the factors affecting Alzheimer's and how to reduce the risk of developing Alzheimer's. A combination of diet and both mental and physical exercise is believed to help in prevention or reducing risk. The book includes:

Discussion on factors in Alzheimer's development

The list of foods that help protect the brain and boost brain health is included in the book:

Over 30 recipes including teas, smoothies, broths, and other dishes that incorporate brain-boosting foods:

References and links to several research studies on Alzheimer's and brain foods.

ALL NATURAL WELLNESS DRINKS

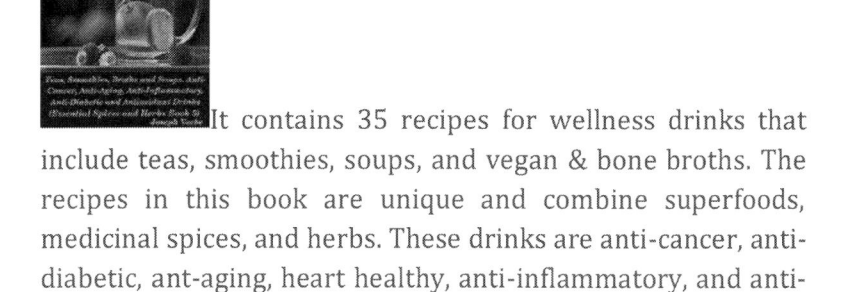

It contains 35 recipes for wellness drinks that include teas, smoothies, soups, and vegan & bone broths. The recipes in this book are unique and combine superfoods, medicinal spices, and herbs. These drinks are anti-cancer, anti-diabetic, ant-aging, heart healthy, anti-inflammatory, and anti-oxidant as well as promote weight loss.

By infusing nature-based nutrients (super fruits and vegetables, spices, and herbs) into drink recipes, we get some amazing wellness drinks that not only replace water loss but nourish the body with vitamins, essential metals, anti-oxidants, and many other nutrients. These drinks may be further enhanced by incorporating spices and herbs along with other superfoods. These drinks not only help heal the body but also enhance the immune system to help prevent many forms of diseases. These drinks may also help rejuvenate the body and delay the aging process. The book also includes suggested wellness drinks for common ailments.

ESSENTIAL SPICES AND HERBS: GINGER

Ginger is a spice known to man for thousands of years and has been used for cooking and as a natural remedy for

CURRY: Curry Powder and Spice Mixes

common ailments. Recent studies have shown that ginger has anti-cancer, anti-inflammatory, and anti-oxidant properties. Ginger helps in reducing muscle pain and is an excellent remedy for nausea. Ginger promotes a healthy digestive system. The book details:

- Many health benefits of ginger including fighting cancer, inflammation, pain and nausea
- Remedies using ginger
- Recipes for teas, smoothies, and other dishes
- References and links to a number of research studies on the effectiveness of ginger

ESSENTIAL SPICES AND HERBS: GARLIC

Garlic is one of the worlds healthiest foods. It helps in maintaining a healthy heart, an excellent remedy for common inflections and has both anti-oxidant and anti-inflammatory properties. It is an excellent food supplement that provides some key vitamins and minerals. This book details the benefits of garlic and describes many easy recipes for incorporating garlic into the diet:

- Many health benefits of garlic including fighting cancer, inflammation, heart health and more
- Remedies using garlic
- Recipes for teas, smoothies, and other dishes
- References and links to a number of research studies on the effectiveness of garlic

ESSENTIAL SPICES AND HERBS: CINNAMON

Cinnamon is an essential spice. It has Anti-diabetic, anti-inflammatory, anti-oxidant, anti-cancer and anti-infections and neuroprotective properties. Cinnamon is a spice known to man for thousands of years and has been used for food preservation, baking, cooking, and as a natural remedy for common ailments. Recent studies have shown that cinnamon has important medicinal properties. This book explains:

- Many health benefits of cinnamon including anti-diabetic, neuroprotective and others.
- Recipes for teas, smoothies, and other dishes
- References and links to a number of research studies on the effectiveness of cinnamon

ANTI-CANCER CURRIES

It is estimated that more than 50% of the cancer incidents are preventable by changing lifestyles, controlling or avoiding cancer-causing factors, or simply eating healthy. There are several foods that are known to have anti-cancer properties either directly or indirectly. Some of these have properties that inhibit cancer cell growth while others have anti-

CURRY: Curry Powder and Spice Mixes

oxidant and anti-inflammatory properties that contribute to overall health. However, many spices and herbs have direct anti-cancer properties and when one uses anti-cancer spices and herbs in cooking fresh food, there is an immense benefit to be gained. Curry dishes are cooked using many spices that have anti-oxidant, anti-inflammatory, and anti-cancer properties.

This book contains 30 curry recipes that use healthy and anti-cancer ingredients. These recipes are simple and take an average of 20-30 minutes to prepare.

BEGINNERS GUIDE TO COOKING WITH SPICES

Have you ever wondered how to cook with spices? Learn about the many benefits of spices and how to cook with them!

Find out how to start using spices as seasoning and healthy foods. Includes sample recipes,

Beginner's guide to cooking with spices is an introductory book that explains the history, various uses, and their medicinal properties and health benefits. The book details how they may be easily incorporated in everyday cooking. The book will cover the following:

- Health benefits of spices and herbs
- Spice mixes from around the world and their uses
- Tips for cooking with Spices
- Cooking Vegan with Spices
- Cooking Meat and Fish with spices
- Spiced Rice Dishes

- Spicy Soups and Broths

Easy Indian Instant Pot Cookbook

Instant Pot or Electric Pressure Cooker is the most important cooking device in my kitchen. It saves me time, energy, and helps me prepare hassle-free Indian meals all the time.

The Easy Indian Instant Pot Meals contains includes:
- Recipes for 50 Indian dishes
- Tips for cooking with Instant Pot or any electric pressure cooker
- General tips for cooking with spices

Fighting the Virus: How to Boost Your Body's Immune Response and Fight Virus Naturally

What can we do to improve our health and immune response so that our bodies are less prone to viral or bacterial infections? How can we enable our body for a speedy recovery in case of getting such infections?

The answer lies in lifestyle changes that include better hygiene practices, exercise, sleep, and a better diet to keep our body in

optimum health. This book is focused on understanding the body's immune system, factors that improve the body's immune response and some natural remedies and recipes. The book contains:
- Overview of the human immune system
- Factors affecting immune response
- Natural substances that fight viral, fungal and bacterial infections
- Recipes that may improve immunity and help speedy recovery
- Supplements that may help improve the immune system
- Scientific studies and references

EASY SPICY EGGS: ALL NATURAL EASY AND SPICY EGG RECIPES

Recipes in this book are not a collection of authentic dishes, but a spicy version of chicken recipes that are easy to make and 100% healthy and flavorful. Ingredients used are mostly natural without any preserved or processed foods.

Most of these recipes include tips and tricks to vary and adapt to your taste of spice level or make with some of the ingredients you like other than the prescribed ingredients in the recipes.

There are about 30 recipes in the book with ideas to make another 30 or even more with the suggestions and notes included with many of the recipes. Cooking does not have to be prescriptive but can be creative. I invite you to try your own variations and apply your creativity to cook dishes that are truly your own.

FOOD FOR THE BRAIN

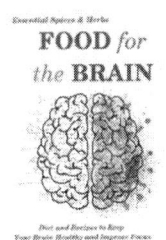

Nature provides for foods that nourish both the body and the brain. Most often the focus of the diet is physical nourishment, - muscle building, weight loss, energy, athletic performance, and many others. Similar to foods that help the body, there are many foods that help the brain, improve memory and help slow down the aging process. While it is normal to have your physical and mental abilities somewhat slow down with age, diseases such as Alzheimer's, and Parkinson's impact these declines even more. Brain function decline accelerates, and more and more brain cells eventually die over time.

With regular exercises, strength training, practicing martial arts and other physical activities can arrest the physical decline. This book's primary focus is on managing decline in mental and brain function through diet and contains the following:
Characteristics of foods that helps in keeping your brain healthy and young. Brain healthy foods including meats, fruits, vegetables, spices, herbs, and seafood. Supplements to improve memory, cognition and support brain health
Mediterranean diet recipe ideas
DASH diet recipe ideas
Asian diet recipe ideas
Brain boosting supplements and recommendations products and dosage
References

Printed in Great Britain
by Amazon